Automotive
Technology
Principles, Diagnosis, and Service

SECOND EDITION

James D. Halderman
Sinclair Community College

Chase D. Mitchell, Jr.
Utah Valley State College

Prentice Hall

Upper Saddle River, New Jersey
Columbus, Ohio

Library of Congress Cataloging-in-Publication Data

Halderman, James D.
   Automotive technology : principles, diagnosis, and service / James D. Halderman,
Chase D. Mitchell, Jr.—2nd ed.
      p. cm.
   ISBN 0-13-099453-7
   1. Automotive—Maintenance and repair. 2. Automobiles—Design and construction. I.
Mitchell, Chase D. II. Title.

TL152 .H25 2003
629.28'72—dc21   2002071470

Editor in Chief: Stephen Helba
Executive Editor: Ed Francis
Production Editor: Christine M. Buckendahl
Design Coordinator: Diane Ernsberger
Cover Designer: Ali Mohrman
Production Manager: Brian Fox
Marketing Manager: Mark Marsden

This book was set in New Century Schoolbook by Carlisle Communications, Ltd., and was printed and bound by Courier
Kendallville, Inc. The cover was printed by Phoenix Color Corp.

Pearson Education Ltd.
Pearson Education Australia Pty. Limited
Pearson Education Singapore Pte. Ltd.
Pearson Education North Asia Ltd.
Pearson Education Canada, Ltd.
Pearson Educación de Mexico, S.A. de C.V.
Pearson Education—Japan
Pearson Education Malaysia Pte. Ltd.
Pearson Education, *Upper Saddle River, New Jersey*

10 9 8 7 6 5
ISBN: 0-13-099453-7

10 9 8 7 6 5 4 3 2 1
School Edition ISBN: 0-13-183693-5

Preface

The 2003 edition of *Automotive Technology: Principles, Diagnosis, and Service* is organized around the eight ASE automobile test areas and is correlated to the NATEF Task List. Terminology throughout the text reflects the SAE J1930 standard.

ASE and NATEF Correlated

This comprehensive textbook is divided into sections that correspond to the eight areas of certification as specified by the National Institute for Automotive Service Excellence (ASE) and the National Automotive Technicians Education Foundation (NATEF). The areas of the ASE material certification test are listed in the objectives at the beginning of each chapter, and all laboratory worksheets are correlated to the NATEF Task List.

Diagnostic Approach

The primary focus of this textbook is to satisfy the need for problem diagnosis. Time and time again, the author has heard that technicians need more training in diagnostic procedures and skill development. To meet this need and to help illustrate how real problems are solved, diagnostic stories are included throughout. Each new topic covers the parts involved plus their purpose, function, and operation, as well as how to test and diagnose each system.

Multimedia System Approach

The multimedia CD-ROM that accompanies and supplements the textbook is informative and also makes learning more fun for the student. The CD includes:

1. Live action videos and animation to help students understand complex systems.
2. A glossary of automotive terms.
3. Sample ASE test questions with immediate correct answer feedback.
4. Sample worksheets.
5. ASE content list for each of the eight ASE areas.
6. NATEF Task Lists for all eight ASE areas.

Internet (World Wide Web) Approach

Included with the book is a coupon that entitles the owner to *free* access to an ASE test preparation Website for an extended time period. Now you can practice and take the ASE certification tests with confidence. Included at this Website are ASE-type questions for each of the eight ASE automotive areas plus sample questions for advanced level engine performance (L1). There are over 2,000 total questions. The questions are presented 10 at a time, then graded (marked). The correct answer is then given as you scroll back through the questions. This feature allows students to study at their own pace.

Worktext Approach

A separate worktext accompanies the book. Each worktext page is correlated to the NATEF Task List. The worksheets included in the worktext help instructors and students apply the material presented to everyday-type activities and typical service and testing procedures. The worksheets show typical results and a listing of what could be defective if the test results are not within the acceptable range. These sheets help build diagnostic and testing skills.

Chapter Components

- Each chapter opens with a list of learning *objectives* including the ASE content area covered by the chapter. These objectives identify the topics covered and goals to be achieved in the chapter.
- Most chapters contain *tech tips, diagnostic stories, frequently asked questions, high-performance tips,* and *safety tips.*
- All chapters contain a *summary* at the end that highlights the material covered in the chapter.
- *Review questions* (discussion-type questions) are offered at the end of each chapter.
- Each chapter contains *ASE certification-type questions.*

Type Styles Used in This Text

Various type styles are used throughout this text to emphasize words, identify important terms, and highlight figure references. *Italic type* is used to emphasize words and terms. For example, the word *not* is often printed in italic type when it is important that an operation be avoided. New terms appear in **bold type** at first usage. These terms are defined when introduced, and most are listed in the glossary at the back of the text.

Troubleshooting Charts

Troubleshooting charts have been added to the end of each service chapter. These charts will help the reader diagnose and repair common problems.

Color Use

Color is used extensively throughout this text to enhance understanding and highlight important information. Hundreds of color photographs help students grasp the subject material.

New Features of the Second Edition

1. All eight areas of ASE and NATEF thoroughly covered and correlated.
2. ASE areas and content areas included in the objectives at the beginning of each chapter.
3. Hundreds of new color photographs and line drawings to help students understand the content material and to bring the subject alive.
4. Expanded electrical and electronic content with an additional three chapters including a chapter on audio systems.
5. Expanded coverage of OBD II and I/M 240.
6. Expanded coverage on manual and automatic transmissions.
7. Many new photo sequences help to explain service procedures.
8. New topics covered include use of digital storage oscilloscopes (DSO) and clamp-on multimeters, to name but two.
9. Each technical topic discussed in one place or chapter. Unlike other textbooks, this book is written so that the theory, construction, diagnosis, and service of a particular component or system is presented in one location. There is no need to search through the entire book for other references to the same topic.
10. Spanish-language glossary.

Instructor Package

A comprehensive *instructor package* is available free when the text is adopted for classroom use from Prentice Hall (call 1-800-526-0485 or visit Prentice Hall online at www.prenhall.com).

This instructor package includes the following:

- PowerPoint presentation on topics covered in the text.
- Instructor CD with suggested student activities, a test bank, photo library with hundreds of digital color photos, as well as many other useful elements for the classroom.
- Answers to all questions in the textbook.
- Companion Website where instructors can obtain additional helpful teaching material and handouts, as well as links that can help students and instructors keep up to date.

■ ACKNOWLEDGMENTS

A large number of people and organizations have cooperated in providing the reference material and technical information used in this text. The authors wish to express sincere thanks to the following organizations for their special contributions:

Accu Industries, Inc.

Allied Signal Automotive Aftermarket

Arrow Automotive

ASE

Autolite Spark Plugs

Automotion, Inc.

Automotive Engine Rebuilders Association (AERA)

Automotive Parts Rebuilders Association (APRA)

Automatic Transmission Rebuilders Association (ATRA)

Battery Council International (BCI)

Bear Automotive

Bendix

British Petroleum (BP)

Cadillac Motor Car Division, General Motors Corporation

Camwerks Corporation

Castrol Incorporated

Champion Spark Plugs, Cooper Automotive, Cooper Industries

Chrysler Corporation

Clayton Associates

Cooper Automotive Company

Dana Corporation, Perfect Circle Products

Defiance Engine Rebuilders, Incorporated

Delphi Chassis, GMC

The Dow Chemical Company

Duralcan USA

EIS Brake Parts

Envirotest Systems Corporation

Fel-Pro Incorporated

Fluke Corporation

FMSI

Ford Motor Company

General Electric Lighting Division

General Motors Corporation Service Technology Group

Goodson Auto Machine Shop Tools and Supplies

Greenlee Brothers and Company

Hennessy Industries

Hunter Engineering Company

Jasper Engines and Transmissions

John Bean Company

Modine Manufacturing Company

Neway

Northstar Manufacturing Company, Inc.

Oldsmobile Division, GMC

Parsons and Meyers Racing Engines

Perfect Hofmann-USA

Raybestos Brake Parts, Inc.

Reynolds and Reynolds Company

Robert Bosch Corporation

Rottler Manufacturing

Shimco International, Inc.

SKF USA, Inc.

Society of Automotive Engineers (SAE)

Speciality Products Company

Sunnen Products Company

Toyota Motor Sales, USA, Inc.

TRW Inc.

Wurth USA, Inc.

Portions of materials contained herein have been reprinted with the permission of General Motors Corporation Service Technology Group.

Technical and Content Reviewers

The following people reviewed the manuscript before production and checked it for technical accuracy and clarity of presentation. Their suggestions and recommendations were included in the final draft of the manuscript. Their input helped make this textbook clear and technically accurate while maintaining the easy-to-read style that has made other books from the same authors so popular.

Jim Anderson
Greenville High School

Victor Bridges
Umpqua Community College

Dr. Roger Donovan
Illinois Central College

A.C. Durdin
Moraine Park Technical College

Herbert Ellinger
Western Michigan University

Al Engledahl
College of Dupage

Larry Hagelberger
Upper Valley Joint Vocational School

Oldrick Hajzler
Red River College

Betsy Hoffman
Vermont Technical College

Steven T. Lee
Lincoln Technical Institute

Carlton H. Mabe, Sr.
Virginia Western Community College

Roy Marks
Owens Community College

Kerry Meier
San Juan College

Fritz Peacock
Indiana Vocational Technical College

Dennis Peter
NAIT (Canada)

Kenneth Redick
Hudson Valley Community College

Mitchell Walker
St. Louis Community College at Forest Park

Photo Sequences

The authors wish to thank Rick Henry, who photographed many of the photo sequences. Most of the sequences were taken in automotive service facilities while live work was being performed. Special thanks to all who helped, including:

BP ProCare
Dayton, Ohio
Tom Brummitt
Jeff Stueve
Bob Babal
Brian Addock
Jason Brown
Don Patton
Dan Kanapp

Rodney Cobb Chevrolet
Eaton, Ohio
Clint Brubacker

Dare Automotive Specialists
Centerville, Ohio
David Schneider
Eric Archdeacon
Jim Anderson

Electric Garage
Dan Forbes

Foreign Car Service
Huber Heights, Ohio
Mike McCarthy
George Thielen
Ellen Finke
Greg Hawke
Bob Massie

Genuine Auto Parts Machine Shop
Dayton, Ohio
Freddy Cochran
Tom Berger

Import Engine and Transmission
Dayton, Ohio
Elias Daoud
James Brown
Robert Riddle
Felipe Delemos
Mike Pence

J and B Transmission Service
Dayton, Ohio
Robert E. Smith
Ray L. Smith
Jerry Morgan
Scott Smith
Daryl Williams
George Timitirou

Saturn of Orem
Orem, Utah

We also wish to thank the faculty and students at Sinclair Community College in Dayton, Ohio, and Utah Valley State College in Orem, Utah, for their ideas and suggestions. Most of all, we wish to thank Michelle Halderman for her assistance in all phases of manuscript preparation.

James D. Halderman
Chase D. Mitchell, Jr.

Automotive Technology

Brief Contents

S E C T I O N   VII

Suspension and Steering   891

S E C T I O N   VIII

Manual Drive Trains and Axles   1017

S E C T I O N   IX

Automatic Transmissions and Transaxles   1147

Contents

S E C T I O N   II

Engine Repair   77

4

Engine Operation, Parts, and Specifications   78

5

Engine Condition Diagnosis   94

6

Engine Disassembly, Cleaning, and Crack Detection   108

12

Engine Assembly and Installation   224

SECTION

Electrical/Electronic Systems   249

13

Electrical and Electronic Principles and Circuits   250

14

Meters, Scopes, Wiring, and Schematics   283

15

Batteries and Battery Testing   332

31

Engine Performance Diagnosis and Testing   695

SECTION VI

Brakes   733

32

Brake System Principles and Operation   734

33

Master Cylinders and the Hydraulic System   746

34

Wheel Bearings and Service   779

35

Drum Brake Operation, Diagnosis, and Service   796

36

Disc Brake Operation, Diagnosis, and Service   815

43

SECTION **VIII**

Manual Drive Trains and Axles 1017

44

45

46

47

48

Four-Wheel Drive and All-Wheel Drive   1122

SECTION

Automatic Transmissions and Transaxles   1147

49

Automatic Transmission/Transaxle Principles   1148

50

Automatic Transmission/Transaxle Diagnosis and Service   1178

APPENDIXES
(Sample ASE Certification Tests)

Tech Tips, Frequently Asked Questions, Diagnostic Stories, High Performance Tips, and Safety Tips

13

Electrical and Electronic Principles and Circuits   250

14

Meters, Scopes, Wiring, and Schematics   283

15

Batteries and Battery Testing   332

16

Cranking System Operation, Diagnosis, and Service   353

17

Charging System Operation, Diagnosis, and Service   377

18

Lighting and Signaling Circuit Operation and Diagnosis   411

19

Dash Instruments Operation and Diagnosis   429

20

Accessory Circuits Operation and Diagnosis   449

21

Audio System Operation and Diagnosis   477

22

Heating, Ventilation, and Air Conditioning Principles   488

23

Heating and Air Conditioning Diagnosis and Service   513

Photo Sequences

Features of This Text

To enhance readability and understanding, as well as making study more enjoyable, this text is packed with many special features.

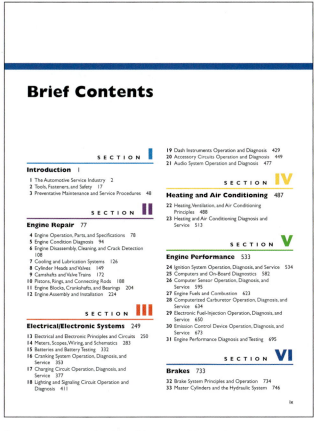

Automotive Technology: Principles, Diagnosis, and Service, 2E, is arranged into nine major sections. The first is an introductory section. The next eight sections correspond to the eight Automotive Service Excellence (ASE) categories.

More than 2200 **photos** and **illustrations,** most in full color, graphically depict critical components and procedures much better than just words could explain. In fact, the illustrations could almost stand alone as a teaching tool.

Photo Sequences show in detail the steps involved in performing a test or service procedure. The Photo Sequences reinforce classroom instruction by allowing students to view the important elements in an automotive procedure as they learn about a particular topic.

Engine Assembly and Installation 243

PHOTO SEQUENCE 11 Valve Adjustment

P11-1 Before starting the process of adjusting the valves, look up the specifications and exact procedures. The technician is checking this information from a computer CD-ROM-based information system.

P11-2 The tools necessary to adjust the valves on an engine with adjustable rocker arms include basic hand tools, feeler gauge, and a torque wrench.

P11-3 An overall view of the four-cylinder engine that is due for a scheduled valve adjustment according to the vehicle manufacturer's recommendations.

P11-4 Start the valve adjustment procedure by first disconnecting and labeling, if necessary, all vacuum lines that need to be removed to gain access to the valve cover.

P11-5 The air intake tube is being removed from the throttle body.

P11-6 With all vacuum lines and the intake tube removed, the valve cover can be removed after removing all retaining bolts.

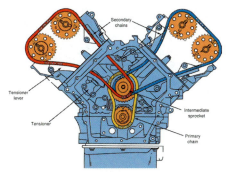

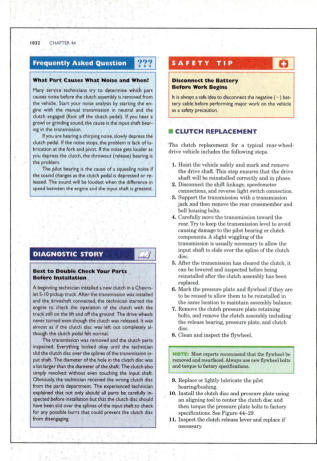

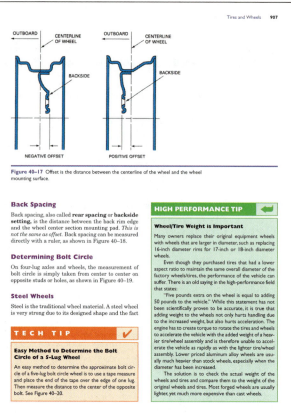

The **Frequently Asked Question** feature was included at the request of students and faculty to provide answers to questions that many students and beginning service technicians have when studying technical automotive topics.

Each **Diagnostic Story** presents a problem or situation that the service technician might face. These stories tell about the steps taken to arrive at a solution to a technical problem.

The **Safety Tip** feature is new to this edition. This feature warns students about possible hazards on the job and how to avoid harm.

Tech Tips help readers gain insight into specific situations that they might encounter on the job and are based on real-life experiences.

High Performance Tips focus on techniques often used in motor sport racing to improve vehicle performance.

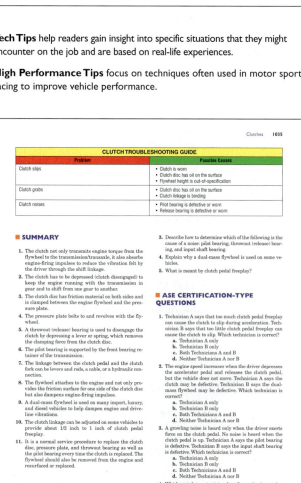

Troubleshooting Guides have been added to the end of each service chapter. These guides help students diagnose and repair common problems. In addition, the **Review Questions** and **ASE Certification-Type Questions** at the end of each chapter will help students gain confidence in their ability to pass ASE tests and achieve the certification they will need to qualify for automotive technician positions in the automotive service industry.

Prentice Hall Multimedia Series in Automotive Technology

Introduction

1   **The Automotive Service Industry**
2   **Tools, Fasteners, and Safety**
3   **Preventative Maintenance and Service Procedures**

The introduction to automotive service includes material needed by the beginning service technician that is beyond what is included under the eight areas of ASE. Chapter 1 describes the various opportunities within the automotive service industry and introduces terms and procedures used throughout the industry. Chapter 2 includes tools and safety. All basic hand tools are shown as well as information on fasteners and the safe methods of hoisting a vehicle. Chapter 3 describes typical preventative maintenance and service procedures.

The Automotive Service Industry

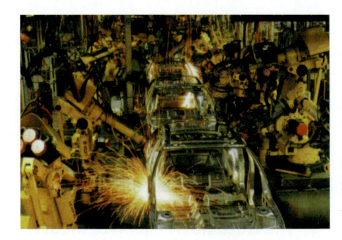

Figure 1–1 Chassis being welded by robotic machinery on an assembly line at Saturn plant. (Courtesy of Saturn Corporation)

The automotive industry is huge. It incorporates new vehicle manufacturing and service as well as maintenance and repair of all of the existing vehicles on the road today.

■ VEHICLE CONSTRUCTION

Vehicles are assembled in factories (also called *plants*) from parts and components manufactured at other factories. For example, a vehicle may use stamped-steel body panels shipped from a steel-stamping company and then welded into a finished body at the assembly plant. See Figure 1–1.

Assembly plants also have subassembly lines where many smaller components are combined into larger components that are eventually assembled to form the finished vehicle. Examples of a subassembly line include:

- Instrument panel and dash assembly
- Steering column assembly
- Engine and transmission/transaxle assembly

Many component parts of a vehicle are assembled before being installed in a vehicle, which is the reason some parts are difficult to remove after the vehicle has been assembled.

■ FRAME CONSTRUCTION

Frame construction usually consists of channel-shaped steel beams welded and/or fastened together.

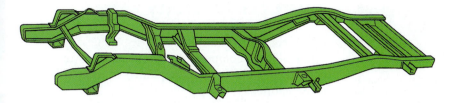

Figure 1–2 Typical frame of a vehicle.

Vehicles with a separate frame and body are usually called body-on-frame vehicles (BOF). Many terms are used to label or describe the frame of a vehicle including:

Ladder Frame

A ladder frame is a common name for a type of perimeter frame where the transverse connecting members are straight across, as in Figure 1–2.

Perimeter Frame

A perimeter frame consists of welded or riveted frame members around the entire perimeter of the body. See Figure 1–3.

Stub-Type Frames

A stub frame is a partial frame often used on unit-body vehicles to support the power train and suspension components. This frame is also called a *cradle* on many front-wheel drive vehicles. See Figure 1–4.

■ UNIT-BODY CONSTRUCTION

Unit-body construction (sometimes called *unibody*) is a design that combines the body with the structure of the frame. The body is composed of many individual stamped-steel panels welded together. The strength of this type of construction lies in the *shape* of the assembly. The typical vehicle uses 300 separate stamped-steel panels that are spot-welded together to form a vehicle's body. See Figure 1–5.

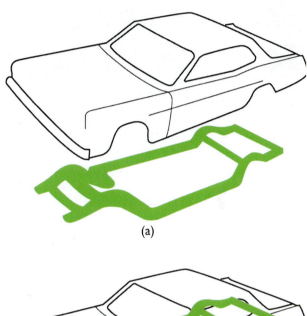

(a)

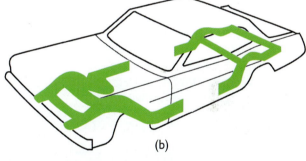

(b)

Figure 1–4 (a) Separate body and frame construction. (b) Unitized construction—the small frame members are for support of the engine and suspension components. Many vehicles attach the suspension components directly to the reinforced sections of the body and do not require the rear frame section.

> **NOTE:** A typical vehicle contains about 10,000 separate individual parts.

■ SPACE-FRAME CONSTRUCTION

Space-frame construction consists of formed sheet steel used to construct a framework of the entire vehicle. The vehicle is driveable without the body, which uses plastic or steel panels to cover the steel framework. See Figure 1–6.

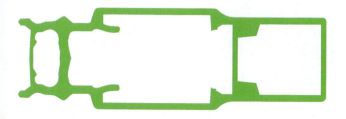

Figure 1–3 Perimeter frame.

Figure 1–5 Note the ribbing and the many different pieces of sheet metal used in the construction of this body.

■ VEHICLE ASSEMBLY

After the body and chassis are constructed, the other vehicle components are assembled to form a completed vehicle. The sequence of assembly usually includes:

1. Attaching the suspension to the frame or subframe
2. Completing the body with the interior, dash, seats, and all wiring
3. Attaching the engine to the frame (if a body-on-frame vehicle) or installing it into the body (if unit-body construction)
4. Attaching all other parts and components such as wheels and tires, front grill, hood, and fenders
5. Starting and driving the completed vehicle off the assembly line into an area where the wheel alignment is checked and adjusted as necessary and then "driving" the vehicle on rollers where it is driven through its normal operating range of gears and speeds while the vehicle computer is checked to be sure everything is okay
6. Loading the vehicles onto rail cars or transport trucks to be delivered to the local new vehicle dealers

Figure 1–6 A Corvette without the body. Notice that the vehicle is complete enough to be driven. This photo was taken at the Corvette Museum in Bowling Green, Kentucky.

■ VEHICLE DEALER PREPARATION

When a new vehicle arrives at the dealership, it must be cleaned and made ready for sale. See Figure 1–7. This process is usually called *new car prep* and involves removing all of the protective plastic and installing the components such as wheel covers, floor mats, etc. that are not installed until the vehicle is ready to sell.

■ VEHICLE SERVICE JOBS

There are many jobs in the vehicle service industry. In smaller service facilities, the duties of many positions may be combined in one job. A large city dealership may have all of the following vehicle service positions.

Service Advisor

A service advisor, also called a **service writer,** is the person at the dealership or service facility designated to communicate the needs of the customer and accurately complete a **repair order.** A repair order is often referred to as an **R.O.** or a **work order.** See Figure 1–8 for an example of a typical R.O. A typical service advisor is not a service technician but is usually a person who can easily talk with people and accurately write on the R.O. exactly what the customer needs or says about how the vehicle is acting. See Figure 1–9. The service advisor's duties include

1. Recording the vehicle identification number (**VIN**) of the vehicle on the R.O.
2. Recording the make, model, year, and mileage on the R.O.
3. Carefully recording what the customer's complaint (concern) is so that the service technician can verify the complaint and make the proper repair
4. Keeping the customer informed as to the progress of the service work

Service Technician

An R.O. is assigned to a technician who is best qualified to perform the work. The technician gets the keys and drives the vehicle to an assigned **service bay** (also called a **stall**), gets the necessary parts from the parts department, and completes the repair. The vehicle is then driven by the service technician to verify the repair.

Shop Foreman

A shop foreman (usually employed in larger dealerships and vehicle repair facilities) is an experienced service technician who is usually paid a salary (so

Figure I–7 Typical new vehicle dealer service department. (Courtesy of Ogle-Tucker Buick)

COST	QUAN.	PART NUMBER / DESCRIPTION	PRICE
	1	Battery Interstate 60 Month Battery	74 00
	1	Oil filter	11 25
	1	Air filter	36 59
	1	Seal Ring	25
	1	Ant Mast	67 97
			190 06

HOME TOWN PONTIAC 8993
100 N. MAIN ST.

NAME: MR CUSTOMER   DATE RECEIVED: 1/9/97
ADDRESS: 444 W. 3rd St.   COMPLETION DATE:
CITY: STATE: ZIP: MILEAGE IN: 52084
VIN: IG2NW51A6SC201   ENGINE NO. 3.1 V-6   MAKE: PONTIAC   MILEAGE OUT:
TYPE OR MODEL: GRAND AM   YEAR: 98   LICENSE NUMBER: BQU449   PHONE WHEN READY: YES ☐ NO ☐
TERMS: ORDER ACCEPTED BY: PHONE:

ALL PARTS ARE NEW UNLESS SPECIFIED OTHERWISE

LABOR CHARGE

LUBRICATE	☐	
CHANGE OIL	☐	
CHANGE OIL FILTER CART.	☐	
CHANGE TRANS. OIL	☐	
CHANGE DIFF. OIL	☐	
PACK FRONT WHEEL BRGS.	☐	
ADJUST BRAKES	☐	
X TIRES	☐	
WASH	☐	
SAFETY INSPECTION	☐	

OPER. NO.	INSTRUCTIONS:	
10	45 K Service	450 00
6	Check Battery Replace	22 50
5	Ant Mast	22 50
5	Check left front Headlight	22 50

SUBLET REPAIRS

GALS. GAS @
QTS. OIL @
LBS. GREASE @

TOTAL GAS - OIL - GREASE

REPLACED PARTS WILL BE RETURNED FOR YOUR INSPECTION. IF YOU DO NOT WANT THEM, PLEASE CHECK THE BLOCK BELOW.
☐ DISCARD REPLACED PARTS

I hereby authorize the repair work herein set forth to be done by you, together with the furnishing by you of the necessary parts and other material for such repair, and agree: that you are not responsible for any delays caused by unavailability or delayed availability of parts or material for any reason; that you neither assume nor authorize any other person to assume for you any liability in connection with such repair; that you shall not be responsible for loss of or damage to the above vehicle, or articles left therein, in case of fire, theft or other cause beyond your control; that an express mechanic's lien is hereby acknowledged on the above vehicle to secure the amount of repairs thereto; that your employees may operate the above vehicle on streets, highways or elsewhere for the purpose of testing and/or inspecting such vehicle. I HEREBY ACKNOWLEDGE RECEIPT OF A COPY HEREOF.

X

ESTIMATE
(UNDER OHIO LAW) YOU HAVE THE RIGHT TO AN ESTIMATE IF THE EXPECTED COST OF REPAIRS OR SERVICES WILL BE MORE THAN TWENTY-FIVE DOLLARS. INITIAL YOUR CHOICE.
___ WRITTEN ESTIMATE   ___ ORAL ESTIMATE
___ I DO NOT REQUEST AN ESTIMATE

DISCLAIMER OF WARRANTIES
THE SELLER, HEREBY EXPRESSLY DISCLAIMS ALL WARRANTIES, EITHER EXPRESSED OR IMPLIED, INCLUDING ANY IMPLIED WARRANTY OF MERCHANTABILITY OR FITNESS FOR A PARTICULAR PURPOSE, AND NEITHER ASSUMES NOR AUTHORIZES ANY OTHER PERSON TO ASSUME FOR IT ANY LIABILITY IN CONNECTION WITH THE SALE OF SAID PRODUCTS.

ORIGINAL ESTIMATE: $ ___
AUTHORIZED ADDITIONS: $ ___
CUSTOMERS ACCEPTANCE: INITIAL HERE ___   DATE ___   TIME ___   BY ___

In the event that you, the customer, authorize commencement but do not authorize completion of a repair or service, a charge will be imposed for disassembly, reassembly or partially completed work. Such charge will be directly related to the actual amount of labor or parts involved in the inspection, repair or service.

	SALE
TOTAL LABOR	517 50
TOTAL PARTS	190 06
GAS, OIL & GREASE	
SUBLET REPAIRS	
	707 56
TAX 6.5%	45 99
TOTAL	753 55

Figure I–8 Typical repair order (RO). (Courtesy of The Reynolds and Reynolds Company)

much a week, month, or year). Typical shop foreman's duties include:

- Test driving the customer's vehicles to verify the customer complaint
- Assigning work to the service technicians
- Assisting the service technicians
- Assisting the service manager
- Verifying that the repair is completed satisfactorily

Service Manager

The service manager rarely works on a vehicle but instead organizes the service facility and keeps it operating smoothly. The service manager typically handles all of the paper work associated with operating a service department. Typical service manager's duties include:

- Establishing guidelines to determine the technician's efficiency

- Supervising any warranty claims submitted to the vehicle manufacturer
- Evaluating and budgeting for shop tools and equipment
- Establishing service department hours of operation and employee schedules
- Assigning working hours and pay for technicians and others in the service department

Parts Manager

The parts manager and other parts personnel such as the parts **counter person** are responsible for getting the correct part for the service technician. The specific duties of a parts manager usually include:

- Ordering parts from the vehicle manufacturers and aftermarket companies
- Organizing the parts department in a clear and orderly fashion
- Developing contacts with parts departments in other local dealerships so that parts that are not

Figure 1–10 A service technician working on the brakes of a vehicle in a new-vehicle dealership service department. (Courtesy of Ogle-Tucker Buick)

Figure 1–9 A service advisor, also called a service writer or service consultant, is the person that greets the customers and prepares the repair order for the service technician. Note that this service advisor is wearing a cordless telephone and is therefore always in touch regardless of where he is in and around the dealership.

in stock can be purchased quickly and at a reasonable cost

■ TECHNICIAN WORK SITES

Service technician work takes place in a variety of work sites including:

New Vehicle Dealerships

Most dealerships handle one or more brands of vehicle, and the technician employed at dealerships usually has to meet minimum training standards. The training is usually provided at no cost to the technician at regional training centers. The dealer usually pays the service technician for the day(s) spent in training as well as provides or pays for transportation, meals, and lodging. See Figure 1–10.

Independent Service Facilities

These small- to medium-size repair facilities usually work on a variety of vehicles. Technicians employed at independent service facilities usually have to depend on aftermarket manufacturers' seminars or the local vocational school or college to keep technically up-to-date. See Figure 1–11.

Figure 1–11 A typical independent service facility. Independent garages often work on a variety of vehicles and perform many different types of vehicle repairs and service. Some independent garages specialize in just one or two areas of service work or in just one or two makes of vehicles.

Mass Merchandiser

Large national chains of vehicle repair facilities are common in most medium- and large-size cities. Some examples of these chains include Sears, Goodyear, Firestone, and NAPA, as shown in Figure 1–12. Technicians employed by these chains usually work on a wide variety of vehicles. Many of the companies have their own local or regional training sites designed to train beginning service technicians and to provide update training for existing technicians.

Specialty Service Facilities

Specialty service facilities usually limit their service work to selected systems or components of the

Figure 1–12 This NAPA parts store also performs service work from the garage area on the side of the building.

vehicle and/or to a particular brand of vehicle. Examples of specialty service facilities include Midas, Speedy, and AAMCO Transmissions. Many of the franchised specialty facilities have their own technician training for both beginning and advanced technicians.

Fleet Facilities

Many city, county, and state governments have their own vehicle service facilities for the maintenance and repair of their vehicles. Service technicians are usually employees of the city, county, or state and are usually paid by the hour rather than on a commission basis.

■ TECHNICIAN PAY METHODS

Straight-Time Pay

When the particular service or repair is not covered or mentioned in a flat-rate guide, it is common practice for the technician to **clock-in** and use the actual time spent on the repair as a basis for payment. The technician uses a flat-rate time ticket and a time clock to record the actual time. Being paid for the actual time spent is often called **straight time** or **clock time.** Difficult engine performance repairs are often calculated using the technician's straight time.

Flat-Rate Pay Methods

Beginning service technicians are usually paid by the hour. The hourly rate can vary greatly depending on the experience of the technician and type of work being performed. Most experienced service technicians are paid by a method called **flat-rate.** The flat-rate method of pay is also called **incentive**

or **commission pay.** "Flat-rate" means that the technician is paid a set amount of time (flat-rate) for every service operation. The amount of time allocated is published in a flat-rate manual. For example, if a bumper requires replacement, the flat-rate manual may call for 1.0 hour (time is always expressed in tenths of an hour). The service technician would therefore get paid one hour of pay regardless of how long it actually took to complete the job. Often, the technician can "beat flat-rate" by performing the operation in less time than the published time. It is therefore important that the technician not waste time and work efficiently to get paid the most for a day's work. The technician also has to be careful to perform the service procedure correctly because if the job needs to be done again due to an error, the technician does the repair at no pay. Therefore, the technician needs to be fast and careful at the same time.

The vehicle manufacturer determines the flat-rate for each labor operation by having a team of technicians perform the operation several times. The average of all of these times is often published as the allocated time. The flat-rate method was originally developed to determine a fair and equitable way to pay dealerships for covered warranty repairs. Because the labor rate differs throughout the country, a fixed dollar amount would not be fair compensation. However, if a time could be established for each operation, then the vehicle manufacturer could reimburse the dealership for the set number of hours multiplied by the labor rate approved for that dealership. For example, if the approved labor rate is $60.00 per hour and:

Technician A performed
$$6.2 \text{ hours} \times \$60.00 = \$372.00$$
Technician B performed
$$4.8 \text{ hours} \times \$60.00 = \$288.00$$
The total paid to the dealership
$$\text{by the manufacturer} = \$660.00$$

This does not mean that the service technician gets paid $60.00 per hour. Sorry, no! This means that the dealership gets reimbursed for labor at the $60.00 per hour rate. The service technician usually gets paid a lot less than half of the total labor charge.

Depending on the part of the country and the size of the dealership and community, the technician's flat-rate per hour income can vary from $7.00 to $20.00 or more per flat-rate hour. Remember, a high pay rate ($20 for example) does not necessarily mean that the service technician will be earning $800.00 per week (40 hours × $20.00 per hour = $800.00). If the dealership is not busy or it is a slow time of year, maybe the technician will only have the opportunity to "turn" 20 hours per week. So it is not really the pay rate that determines what a technician will earn but rather a combination of all of the following:

- Pay rate
- Number of service repairs performed
- Skill and speed of the service technician
- Type of service work (a routine brake service may be completed faster and more easily than a difficult engine performance problem)

A service technician earns more at a busy dealership with a lower pay rate than at a smaller or less busy dealership with a higher pay rate.

Customer Pay

Customer pay (CP) means that the customer will be paying for the service work at a dealership rather than the warranty. Often the same factory flat-rate number of hours is used to calculate the technician's pay, but customer pay often pays the service technician at a higher rate. For example, a service technician earning $15.00 per flat-rate hour for warranty work may be paid $18.00 per hour for customer-pay work. Obviously, service technicians prefer to work on vehicles that require customer-pay service work rather than factory-warranty service work.

Nondealership Flat-Rate

Technicians who work for independent service facilities or at other nondealership locations use one or both of the following to set rates of pay:

- *Mitchell Parts and Time Guide*
- *Motors Parts and Time Guide*

Both of these guides contain service operation and flat-rate times. Generally, these are about 20% higher (longer) than those specified by the factory flat rate to compensate for rust or corrosion and other factors of time and mileage that often lengthen the time necessary to complete a repair. Again, the service technician is usually paid a dollar amount per flat-rate hour based on one of these aftermarket flat-rate guides. The guides also provide a list price for the parts for each vehicle. This information allows the service advisor to accurately estimate the total cost of the repair.

Additional Service Technician Benefits

Many larger dealerships and service facilities often offer some or all of the following:

- Paid uniforms/cleaning
- Vacation time

- Update training (especially new vehicle dealerships)
- Some sort of retirement (usually a contributing 401(k)) program
- Health and dental insurance (usually not fully paid)
- Discounts on parts and vehicles purchased at the dealership or shop

Not all service facilities offer all of these additional benefits.

■ FLAGGING AN R.O.

When a service technician completes a service procedure or repair, a sticker is completed indicating the following:

- Technician number (number rather than a name is often used not only to shorten the identification but also to shield the actual identity of the technician from the customer)
- R.O. number
- Amount of time allocated to the repair expressed in hours and tenths of an hour

The application of the service technician's sticker to the back of the R.O. is often called **flagging the R.O.**

NOTE: The actual assignment of the time is often done by another person at the dealership or service facility. This procedure assures that the correct number of hours is posted to the R.O. and to the technician's ticket.

SUBLET REPAIRS

Often a repair (or a part of a repair) is performed by another person or company outside the dealership or service facility. For example, an engine needing repair that also has a defective or leaking radiator would be repaired by the original repair facility, but the radiator may be sent to a specialty radiator repair shop. The radiator repair cost is then entered on the R.O. as a sublet repair.

PARTS REPLACEMENT

Parts replacement is often called **R & R,** meaning **remove and replace.**

NOTE: R & R can also mean **remove and repair,** but this meaning is generally not used as much now as it used to be when components such as starters and air conditioning compressors were repaired rather than replaced as an assembly.

R & I is often used to indicate **remove and inspect** to check a component for damage. The old replaced part is often returned for remanufacturing and is called a **core.** A **core charge** is often charged by parts stores when a new (or remanufactured) part is purchased. This core charge usually represents the value of the old component. Because it is needed by the remanufacturer as a starting point for the remanufacturing process, the core charge is also an incentive to return the old part for credit (or refund) of the core charge.

Original Equipment Parts

Parts at a new vehicle dealership come either directly from the vehicle manufacturer or a regional dealership. If one dealership purchases from another dealership, the cost of the part is higher, but no waiting is required. If a dealership orders a part from the manufacturer directly, the cost is lower, but there is often a seven- to ten-day waiting period. **Original equipment** parts, abbreviated **OE,** are generally of the highest quality because they have to meet performance and durability standards not required of replacement parts manufacturers.

NOTE: Many service technicians will use only OE parts for certain critical systems such as fuel injection and ignition system components because, in their experience, even though the price is often higher, the extra quality seems to be worth the cost not only to the owner of the vehicle but also to the service technician, who does not have to worry about having to replace the same part twice.

Aftermarket Parts

Parts manufactured to be sold for use after the vehicle is made are often referred to as **aftermarket parts** or **renewal parts.** Most aftermarket parts are sold at automotive parts stores or **jobbers.** A jobber or parts retailer usually gets parts from a large regional **warehouse distributor.** The warehouse distributor can either purchase parts directly from the manufacturer or from an even larger central warehouse. Because each business needs to make a profit (typically, 35%), the cost to the end user may not be lower than it is for the same part purchased at a dealership (a two-step process instead of the typical three-step process) even though it costs more to manufacture the original equipment part. To determine what a 35% margin increase is for any product, simply divide the cost by 0.65. To illustrate how this works, look at the chart below and compare the end cost of a part (part A) from a dealership and a parts store.

NOTE: The cost of the part to the customer where service work is performed is increased about 35% over the base cost of the part. For example, a part that cost the repair facility $40.23 will be billed to the customer at about $61.00. The retail service customer at the dealer may pay $59.17 ($38.46 ÷ 0.65 = $59.17).

New Versus Remanufactured Parts

New parts are manufactured from raw materials and have never been used on a vehicle. A remanu-

Retail Parts Store	New Vehicle Dealership
Manufacturer's selling price = $17.00	Manufacturer's selling price = $25.00
Warehouse distributor's selling price = $26.15 ($17.00 ÷ 0.65 = $26.15)	Parts department selling price = $38.46 ($25.00 ÷ 0.65 = $38.46)
Retail store selling price = $40.23 ($26.15 ÷ 0.65 = $40.23)	

factured component (also called **rebuilt**) has been used on a vehicle until the component wore out or failed. A remanufacturer totally disassembles the component, cleans, machines, and performs all the necessary steps to restore the part to a "like new" look and function. If properly remanufactured, the component can be expected to deliver the same length of service as a new component part.

The cost of a remanufactured component is often less than the cost of a new part.

> **CAUTION:** Do not always assume that a remanufactured component is less expensive than a new component. Due to the three-step distribution process, the final cost to the end user (you) may be close to the same!

Used Parts

Used parts offer another alternative to either new or remanufactured parts. The cost of a used component is typically one-half the cost of the component if purchased new. Wrecking and salvage yards use a Hollander manual that lists original equipment part numbers and cost and cross-references them to other parts that are the same.

■ TECHNICIAN CERTIFICATION

Even though individual franchises and companies often certify their own technicians, there is a nationally recognized certificate organization, the **National Institute for Automotive Service Excellence,** better known by its abbreviation, **ASE.** See Figure 1–13.

There are eight automotive certifications including:

1. Engine Repair (A1) ASE Task List

Content Area	Questions in Test	Percentage of Test
A. General Engine Diagnosis	17	24%
B. Cylinder Head and Valve Train Diagnosis and Repair	18	26%
C. Engine Block Diagnosis and Repair	18	26%
D. Lubrication and Cooling Systems Diagnosis and Repair	9	13%
E. Fuel, Electrical, Ignition and Exhaust Systems Inspection and Service	8	11%
Total	**70**	**100%**

Figure 1–13 The ASE logo. ASE is an abbreviation for the National Institute for Automotive Service Excellence. (Courtesy of ASE)

2. Automatic Transmission/Transaxle (A2) ASE Task List

Content Area	Questions in Test	Percentage of Test
A. General Transmission/Transaxle Diagnosis **1.** Mechanical/Hydraulic Systems (11) **2.** Electronic Systems (14)	25	50%
B. Transmission/Transaxle Maintenance and Adjust.	5	10%
C. In-Vehicle Transmission/Transaxle Repair	9	18%
D. Off-Vehicle Transmission/Transaxle Repair **1.** Removal, Disassembly, and Assembly (3) **2.** Gear Train, Shafts, Bushings, Oil Pump, and Case (4) **3.** Friction and Reaction Units (4)	11	22%
Total	**50**	**100%**

3. Manual Drive Train and Axles (A3) ASE Task List

Content Area	Questions in Test	Percentage of Test
A. Clutch Diagnosis and Repair	6	15%
B. Transmission Diagnosis and Repair	6	15%
C. Transaxle Diagnosis and Repair	8	20%
D. Drive (Half) Shaft and Universal Joint/Constant Velocity (CV) Joint Diagnosis and Repair (Front and Rear Wheel Drive)	6	15%

E. Rear Axle Diagnosis and Repair
  1. Ring and Pinion Gears (3)
  2. Differential Case Assembly (2)
  3. Limited Slip Differential (1)
  4. Axle Shafts (1)
	7	17%

F. Four-Wheel Drive Component Diagnosis and Repair	7	17%
Total	**50**	**100%**

4. Suspension and Steering (A4) ASE Task List

Content Area	Questions in Test	Percentage of Test

A. Steering Systems Diagnosis and Repair
  1. Steering Columns and Manual Steering Gears (3)
  2. Power-Assisted Steering Units (4)
  3. Steering Linkage (3)
	10	25%

B. Suspension Systems Diagnosis and Repair
  1. Front Suspensions (6)
  2. Rear Suspensions (5)
  3. Miscellaneous Service (2)
	13	33%

C. Wheel Alignment Diagnosis, Adjustment, and Repair	12	30%
D. Wheel and Tire Diagnosis and Repair	5	12%
Total	**40**	**100%**

5. Brakes (A5) ASE Task List

Content Area	Questions in Test	Percentage of Test

A. Hydraulic System Diagnosis and Repair
  1. Master Cylinders (non-ABS) (3)
  2. Fluids, Lines, and Hoses (3)
  3. Valves and Switches (non-ABS) (4)
  4. Bleeding, Flushing, and Leak Testing (non-ABS) (4)
	14	25%

B. Drum Brake Diagnosis and Repair	6	11%
C. Disc Brake Diagnosis and Repair	13	24%
D. Power Assist Units Diagnosis and Repair	4	7%
E. Miscellaneous Diagnosis and Repair	7	13%
F. Antilock Brake System Diagnosis and Repair	11	20%
Total	**55**	**100%**

6. Electrical Systems (A6) ASE Task List

Content Area	Questions in Test	Percentage of Test
A. General Electrical/Electronic System Diagnosis	13	26%
B. Battery Diagnosis and Service	4	8%
C. Starting System Diagnosis and Repair	5	10%
D. Charging System Diagnosis and Repair	5	10%

E. Lighting Systems Diagnosis and Repair
  1. Headlights, Parking Lights, Taillights, Dash Lights, and Courtesy Lights (3)
  2. Stoplights, Turn Signals, Hazard Lights, and Back-Up Lights (3)
	6	12%

F. Gauges, Warning Devices, and Driver Information Systems Diagnosis and Repair	6	12%
G. Horn and Wiper/Washer Diagnosis and Repair	3	6%

	Questions in Test	Percentage of Test
H. Accessories Diagnosis and Repair	8	16%
1. Body (4)		
2. Miscellaneous (4)		
Total	**50**	**100%**

7. Heating and Air Conditioning (A7) ASE Task List

Content Area	Questions in Test	Percentage of Test
A. A/C System Diagnosis and Repair 12	24%	
B. Refrigeration System Component Diagnosis and Repair		
1. Compressor and Clutch (5)	10	20%
2. Evaporator, Condenser, and Related Components (5)		
C. Heating and Engine Cooling Systems Diagnosis and Repair	5	10%
D. Operating Systems and Related Controls Diagnosis and Repair		
1. Electrical (8)	16	32%
2. Vacuum/Mechanical (4)		
3. Automatic and Semi-Automatic Heating, Ventilating, and A/C Systems (4)		
E. Refrigerant Recovery, Recycling, and Handling	7	14%
Total	**50**	**100%**

8. Engine Performance (A8) ASE Task List

Content Area	Questions in Test	Percentage of Test
A. General Engine Diagnosis	12	17%
B. Ignition System Diagnosis and Repair	12	17%
C. Fuel, Air Induction, and Exhaust Systems Diagnosis and Repair	13	19%
D. Emissions Control Systems Diagnosis and Repair	10	14%
1. Positive Crankcase Ventilation (1)		
2. Exhaust Gas Recirculation (3)		

Content Area	Questions in Test	Percentage of Test
3. Exhaust Gas Treatment (3)		
4. Evaporative Emissions Controls (3)		
E. Computerized Engine Controls Diagnosis and Repair	19	27%
F. Engine Electrical Systems Diagnosis and Repair	4	6%
1. Battery (1)		
2. Starting System (1)		
3. Charging System (2)		
Total	**70**	**100%**

SAFETY TIP

Infection Control Precautions

Working on a vehicle can result in personal injury, including the possibility of being cut or hurt enough to cause bleeding. Some infections such as hepatitis B, HIV (which can cause acquired immunodeficiency syndrome (AIDS), hepatitis C virus, and others are transmitted in the blood. These infections are commonly called **blood-born pathogens.** Report any injury that involves blood to your supervisor and take the necessary precautions to avoid coming in contact with blood from another person.

To become certified by ASE, the service technician must have two years of experience and pass a test in each area. If a technician passes all eight automotive certification tests, then the technician is considered a master certified automobile service technician. Tests are administered twice a year, in May and again in November. Registration and payment are required to be sent in with payment in early April for the May test and in early October for the November test. Test results are mailed to your home or work address about six to eight weeks after the test(s) is taken.

■ CERTIFICATION IN CANADA

In Canada, in all provinces and territories but Quebec and British Columbia, an Inter-Provincial (IP) Certificate is required. An apprenticeship program is in place that takes a minimum of four years, combining ten months in a shop and about two months in school training in each of the four years. Most apprentices must undergo 7200 hours of training before they can complete the IP examination. ASE certifications are currently used on a voluntary basis

TECH TIP

Work Habit Hints

The following statements reflect the expectations of service managers or shop owners for their technicians:

1. Report to work every day on time. Being several minutes early every day is an easy way to show your service manager and fellow technicians that you are serious about your job and career.
2. If you *must* be late or absent, call your service manager as soon as possible.
3. Keep busy. If not assigned to a specific job, ask what activities the service manager or supervisor wants you to do.
4. Report any mistakes or accidents *immediately* to your supervisor or team leader. *Never* allow a customer to be the first to discover a mistake.
5. Never lie to your employer or to a customer.
6. Always return any borrowed tools as soon as you are done with them and in *clean* condition. *Show* the person you borrowed the tools from that you are returning them to the toolbox or workbench.
7. Keep your work area neat and orderly.
8. Always use fender covers when working under the hood.
9. Double check your work to be sure that everything is correct.

a. Remember: "If you are forcing something, you are probably doing something wrong."
b. Ask for help if unclear as to what to do or how to do it.
10. Do not smoke in a customer's vehicle.
11. Avoid profanity.
12. DO NOT TOUCH THE RADIO! If the radio is turned on and prevents you from hearing noises, turn the volume down. Try to return the vehicle to the owner with the radio at the same volume as originally set.

NOTE: Some shops have a policy that requires employees to turn the radio off.

13. Keep yourself neatly groomed including:
    a. Shirt tail tucked into pants
    b. Daily bathing and use of deodorant
    c. Clean hair, regular haircuts, and hair tied back if long
    d. Men: daily shave or keep beard and/or mustache neatly trimmed
    e. Women: make-up and jewelry kept to a minimum

---

since 1993, however an IP Certificate is still required. Other licensing of automotive technicians may be required in some cases, such as environmental substances, liquefied petroleum gas, or steam operators.

NOTE: A valid driver's license is a must for any automotive service technician.

■ TYPES OF JOBS IN THE AUTOMOTIVE SERVICE INDUSTRY

There is a wide variety of jobs in the automotive service industry depending on the type of service facility.

New Vehicle Dealerships

- New vehicle preparation duties usually include:
  1. Removing plastic protective coverings
  2. Washing the vehicle
  3. Installing roof racks, running boards, or other add-on or dealer-installed options
- Routine service technician duties usually include:
  1. Changing oil and oil filters
  2. Lubricating the chassis
  3. Checking tire pressure
  4. Helping other service technicians
- Used vehicle technician duties usually include:
  1. Repairing all types of faults including interior and mechanical components
  2. Cleaning or detailing the exterior and interior of a vehicle
  3. Performing routine service checks
- Specialist (journey-level) technician (experienced service technician) duties are limited only by the knowledge, skills, and interests of the technician. In larger dealerships, there may be specialists in the following areas:
  1. Engine repair
  2. Automatic transmissions
  3. Steering, suspension, and alignment
  4. Electrical
  5. Engine performance and driveability
  6. Other areas that may be seasonal such as air conditioning

T E C H   T I P

How to Become an Entrepreneur

An entrepreneur is a person who organizes and manages his or her own business, assuming the risk for the sake of a profit. Many service technicians have the desire to own their own repair facility. The wise business owner (entrepreneur) seeks the advice of the following people when starting and operating a business.

- **Attorney (lawyer)**—This professional will help guide you to make sure that your employees and your customers are protected by community, state, and federal regulations.
- **Accountant**—This professional will help you with the journals and records that must be kept by all businesses and help you with elements such as payroll taxes, unemployment taxes, and workmen's compensation that all businesses have to pay.
- **Insurance agent**—This professional will help you select the coverage needed to protect you and your business from major losses.

Independent Service Facilities

Because the work at independent service facilities involves many different types of work on a wide variety of vehicles, the beginning technician is usually assigned routine service procedures that can be quickly learned and mastered, such as

- Oil and oil filter changes
- Tire repair, mounting, balancing, and rotation
- Assisting other technicians performing a wide variety of service work

■ PAYROLL TAXES AND DEDUCTIONS

Gross earnings are the total amount you earned during the pay period. The paycheck you receive will be for an amount called **net** earnings. Taxes and deductions that are taken from your paycheck may include all or most of the following:

- Federal income tax
- State income tax (not all states)
- Social Security taxes (labeled **FICA,** which stands for Federal Insurance Contribution Act)
- Health/dental/eye insurance deductions

In addition to the above, uniform costs, savings plan deductions, parts account deductions, as well as weekly payments for tools, may also reduce the amount of your net or "take home" pay.

■ SUMMARY

1. Vehicle designs include frame, unit-body, and space-frame construction. A full-frame vehicle is often stronger and quieter and permits the towing of heavier loads. Unit-body and space-frame designs are often lighter and more fuel efficient.
2. Vehicle assembly does not necessarily follow the same sequence as would be followed by a service technician while servicing a vehicle. For example, during assembly the engine is usually attached to the chassis before the body is attached. In the field, it is normal for the engine to be removed from a vehicle without having to remove the body.
3. The service advisor writes down what service work the customer says is needed on a repair order, commonly abbreviated R.O.
4. A service technician performs the service work as specified on the repair order.
5. A shop foreman is usually the most highly skilled technician in the shop and is usually assigned to help other technicians and the service manager.
6. A service manager handles all personnel and organizational details of the service facility.
7. Service technicians can work in new vehicle dealerships, independent service facilities, mass merchandisers, specialty service facilities, or fleet facilities.
8. Service technicians are usually paid by the hour (sometimes called *straight time*), on commission, or by the flat-rate method. The flat-rate method pays the service technician a fixed amount for each repair regardless of how long it actually takes to complete.
9. Parts replacement is often called R & R, meaning *remove and replace*.
10. The National Institute for Automotive Service Excellence, usually abbreviated ASE, sets the internationally known standards for vehicle service technician certification.
11. Service work varies depending on the type of business (dealership, independent garage, etc.) as well as the skill level of the technician.

■ REVIEW QUESTIONS

1. Describe the type of vehicle construction that would be best to have for towing a large trailer and explain why.
2. List the steps that are followed to assemble a new body-on-frame vehicle.
3. List the duties of the service advisor.
4. Explain the difference in duties between a shop foreman and the service manager.
5. Describe how a service technician gets paid on the flat-rate pay plan.

■ ASE CERTIFICATION-TYPE QUESTIONS

1. Technician A says that the engine should be removed from the vehicle exactly opposite to the way it was installed during manufacture. Technician B says many vehicles are built without a separate frame. Which technician is correct?
   - **a.** Technician A only
   - **b.** Technician B only
   - **c.** Both Technicians A and B
   - **d.** Neither Technician A nor B

2. A customer explains what needs to be serviced to the _____.
   - **a.** Shop foreman
   - **b.** Service manager
   - **c.** Service advisor
   - **d.** Service technician

3. Two beginning technicians are discussing the flat-rate pay method. Technician A says that the plan pays the same hourly rate regardless of the type of job. Technician B says that the pay plan pays a certain amount of time depending on the job and that the time is multiplied by the rate per hour. Which technician is correct?
   - **a.** Technician A only
   - **b.** Technician B only
   - **c.** Both Technicians A and B
   - **d.** Neither Technician A nor B

4. The customer usually only talks to the _____.
   - **a.** Shop foreman
   - **b.** Service manager
   - **c.** Service advisor
   - **d.** Service technician

5. Technician A says that new vehicle dealers only work on new vehicles. Technician B says that independent service facilities only work on certain vehicles or particular parts of the vehicle such as the transmission. Which technician is correct?
   - **a.** Technician A only
   - **b.** Technician B only
   - **c.** Both Technicians A and B
   - **d.** Neither Technician A nor B

6. Midas, Speedy, and AMMCO are examples of _____.
   - **a.** An independent service facility
   - **b.** A mass merchandiser
   - **c.** A specialty service facility
   - **d.** A fleet facility

7. A service technician performs a brake repair that has a 4.0 hour flat rate. The shop charges $60.00 per hour. Technician A says that the customer will be charged $240.00 for labor plus parts. Technician B says that the service technician will be paid for only 4 hours of work even if the job takes longer. Which technician is correct?
   - **a.** Technician A only
   - **b.** Technician B only
   - **c.** Both Technicians A and B
   - **d.** Neither Technician A nor B

8. Two beginning technicians are discussing how much a flat-rate service technician who works 40 hours but is able to accomplish 50 flat-rate hours of work will be paid. Technician A says that the technician will be paid 40 hours pay. Technician B says the technician will be paid 40 hours pay plus 10 hours of overtime pay. Which technician is correct?
   - **a.** Technician A only
   - **b.** Technician B only
   - **c.** Both Technicians A and B
   - **d.** Neither Technician A nor B

9. Customer pay usually pays more to the service technician than does warranty work.
   - **a.** True
   - **b.** False

10. ASE technician certification tests are only given twice a year in _____.
    - **a.** May and November
    - **b.** April and October
    - **c.** March and September
    - **d.** December and June

Tools, Fasteners, and Safety

■ THREADED FASTENERS

Most of the threaded fasteners used on engines are cap screws. They are called **cap screws** when they are threaded into a casting. Automotive service technicians usually refer to these fasteners as **bolts,** regardless of how they are used. In this chapter, they are called bolts. Sometimes, studs are used for threaded fasteners. A **stud** is a short rod with threads on both ends. Often, a stud will have coarse threads on one end and fine threads on the other end. The end of the stud with coarse threads is screwed into the casting. A nut is used on the opposite end to hold the parts together. See Figure 2–1.

The fastener threads *must* match the threads in the casting or nut. The threads may be measured either in fractions of an inch (called fractional) or in metric units. The size is measured across the outside of the threads, called the **crest** of the thread.

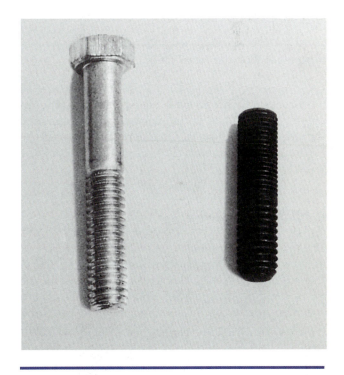

Figure 2–1 Typical bolt on the left and stud on the right. Note the different thread pitch on the top and bottom portions of the stud.

Fractional threads are either coarse or fine. The coarse threads are called Unified National Coarse (UNC), and the fine threads are called Unified National Fine (UNF). Standard combinations of sizes and number of threads per inch (called **pitch**) are used. Pitch can be measured with a thread pitch gauge as shown in Figure 2–2. Bolts are identified by their diameter and length as measured from below the head as shown in Figure 2–3.

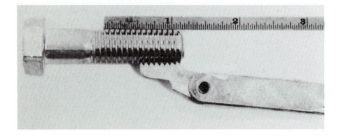

Figure 2–2 Thread pitch gauge used to measure the pitch of the thread. This is a ½-inch-diameter bolt with 13 threads to the inch (½-13).

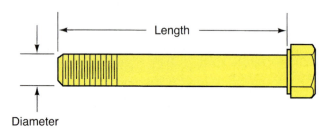

Figure 2–3 Bolt size identification.

Fractional thread sizes are specified by the diameter in fractions of an inch and the number of threads per inch. Typical UNC thread sizes would be ⁵⁄₁₆-18 and ½-13. Similar UNF thread sizes would be ⁵⁄₁₆-24 and ½-20.

■ METRIC BOLTS

The size of a metric bolt is specified by the letter M followed by the diameter in millimeters (mm) across the outside (crest) of the threads. Typical metric sizes would be M8 and M12. Fine metric threads are specified by the thread diameter followed by X and the distance between the threads measured in millimeters (M8 X 1.5).

■ GRADES OF BOLTS

Bolts are made from many different types of steel, and for this reason some are stronger than others. The strength or classification of a bolt is called the **grade.** The bolt heads are marked to indicate their grade strength. Fractional bolts have lines on the head to indicate the grade, as shown in Figures 2–5 and 2–6.

The actual grade of bolts is two more than the number of lines on the bolt head. Metric bolts have a decimal number to indicate the grade. More lines or a higher grade number indicate a stronger bolt. In some cases, nuts and machine screws have similar grade markings.

Figure 2–4 Synthetic wintergreen oil can be used as a penetrating oil to loosen rusted bolts or nuts.

TECH TIP

The Wintergreen Oil Trick

Synthetic wintergreen oil, available at drugstores everywhere, makes an excellent penetrating oil. So the next time you can't get that rusted bolt loose, head for the drugstore. See Figure 2–4.

TECH TIP

A ½-Inch Wrench Does Not Fit a ½-Inch Bolt

A common mistake made by persons new to the automotive field is to think that the size of a bolt or nut is the size of the head. The size of the bolt or nut (outside diameter of the threads) is usually smaller than the size of the wrench or socket that fits the head of the bolt or nut. Examples are given in the following table:

Wrench Size	Thread Size
⁷⁄₁₆ in.	¼ in.
½ in.	⁵⁄₁₆ in.
⁹⁄₁₆ in.	⅜ in.
⅝ in.	⁷⁄₁₆ in.
¾ in.	½ in.
10 mm	6 mm
12 mm or 13 mm*	8 mm
14 mm or 17 mm*	10 mm

*European (Système International d'Unités-SI) metric.

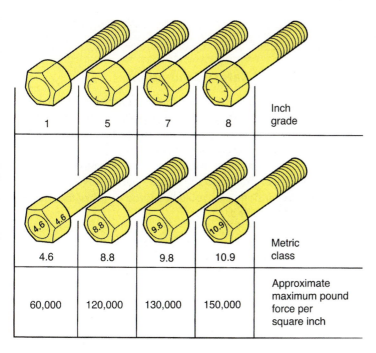

Figure 2–5 Typical bolt (cap screw) grade markings and approximate strength.

1	5	7	8	Inch grade
4.6	8.8	9.8	10.9	Metric class
60,000	120,000	130,000	150,000	Approximate maximum pound force per square inch

Figure 2–6 Every shop should have an assortment of high quality bolts and nuts to replace those damaged during vehicle service procedures.

CAUTION: *Never* use hardware store (nongraded) bolts, studs, or nuts on any vehicle steering, suspension, or brake component. Always use the exact size and grade of hardware that is specified and used by the vehicle manufacturer.

■ NUTS

Most nuts used on cap screws have the same hex size as the cap screw head. Some inexpensive nuts use a hex size larger than the cap screw head. Metric nuts are often marked with dimples to show their strength. More dimples indicate stronger nuts. Some nuts and cap screws use interference fit threads to keep them from accidentally loosening. This means that the shape of the nut is slightly distorted or that a section of the threads is deformed. Nuts can also be kept from loosening with a nylon washer fastened in the nut or with a nylon patch or strip on the threads. See Figure 2–7.

NOTE: Most of these "locking nuts" are grouped together and are commonly referred to as prevailing torque nuts. This means that the nut will hold its tightness or torque and not loosen with movement or vibration. Most prevailing torque nuts should be replaced whenever removed to ensure that the nut will not loosen during service. Always follow manufacturer's recommendations. Anaerobic sealers, such as Loctite, are used on the threads where the nut or cap screw must be both locked and sealed.

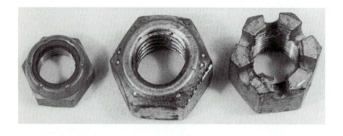

Figure 2–7 Types of lock nuts. On the left, a nylon ring; in the center, a distorted shape; and on the right, a castle for use with a cotter key.

■ WASHERS

Washers are often used under cap screw heads and under nuts. Plain flat washers are used to provide an even clamping load around the fastener. Lock washers are added to prevent accidental loosening. In some accessories, the washers are locked onto the nut to provide easy assembly.

■ BASIC TOOL LIST

Hand tools are used to turn fasteners (bolts, nuts, and screws). The following is a list of hand tools every automotive technician should possess. Specialty tools are not included. See Figures 2–10 through 2–34.

Tool chest
¼-inch drive socket set
¼-inch drive ratchet
¼-inch drive 2-inch extension
¼-inch drive 6-inch extension
¼-inch drive handle
⅜-inch drive socket set
⅜-inch drive Torx set
⅜-inch drive ¹³⁄₁₆-inch plug socket
⅜-inch drive ⅝-inch plug socket
⅜-inch drive ratchet
⅜-inch drive 1 ½-inch extension
⅜-inch drive 3-inch extension
⅜-inch drive 6-inch extension
⅜-inch drive 18-inch extension
⅜-inch drive universal
½-inch drive socket set
½-inch drive ratchet
½-inch drive breaker bar

½-inch drive 5-inch extension
½-inch drive 10-inch extension
⅜-inch to ¼-inch adapter
½-inch to ⅜-inch adapter
⅜-inch to ½-inch adapter
⅜-through 1-inch combo wrench set
10 millimeters through 19 millimeters combo wrench set
¹⁄₁₆-inch through ¼-inch hex wrench set
2 millimeters through 12 millimeters hex wrench set
⅜-inch hex socket
13 millimeters to 14 millimeters flare nut wrench
15 millimeters to 17 millimeters flare nut wrench
⁵⁄₁₆-inch to ⅜-inch flare nut wrench
⁷⁄₁₆-inch to ½-inch flare nut wrench
½-inch to ⁹⁄₁₆-inch flare nut wrench
Diagonal pliers
Needle pliers
Adjustable-jaw pliers
Locking pliers
Snap-ring pliers
Stripping or crimping pliers
Ball-peen hammer
Rubber hammer
Dead-blow hammer
Five-piece standard screwdriver set
Four-piece Phillips screwdriver set
#15 Torx screwdriver
#20 Torx screwdriver
Crowfoot set (fractional inch)
Crowfoot set (metric)
Awl

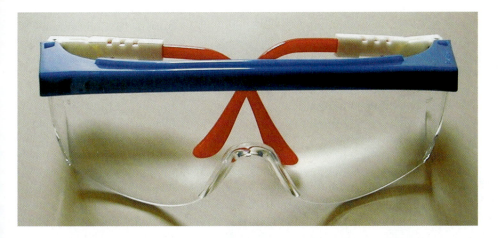

Figure 2–8 Safety glasses should be worn at all times when working on or around any vehicle or servicing any component.

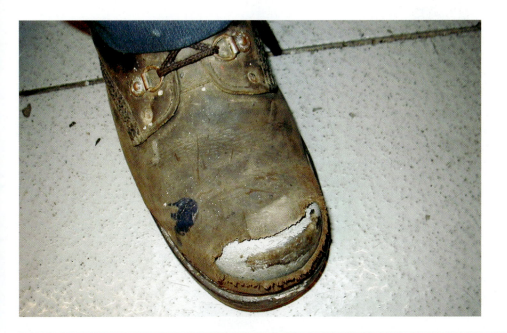

Figure 2–9 Steel-toed shoes are a worthwhile investment to help prevent foot injury due to falling objects. Even these well-worn shoes can protect the feet of this service technician.

Mill file	Filter wrench (smaller filters)
Center punch	Safety glasses
Pin punches (assorted sizes)	Circuit tester
Chisel	Feeler gauge
Utility knife	Scraper
Valve core tool	Pinch bar
Coolant tester	Sticker knife
Filter wrench (large filters)	Magnet

Figure 2–10 Combination wrench. The openings are the same size at both ends. Notice the angle of the open end to permit use in close spaces.

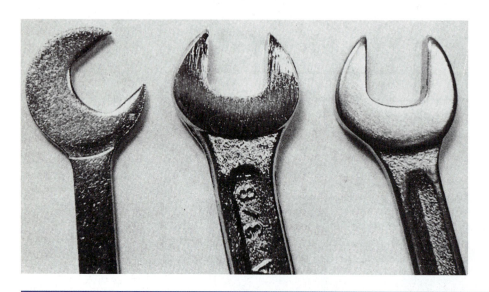

Figure 2–11 Three different qualities of open-end wrenches. The cheap wrench on the left is made from weaker steel and is thicker and less accurately machined than the standard in the center. The wrench on the right is of professional quality (and price).

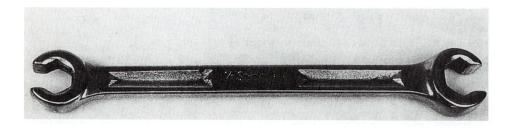

Figure 2–12 Flare-nut wrench. Also known as a *line wrench*, *fitting wrench*, or *tube-nut wrench*. This style of wrench is designed to grasp most of the flats of a six-sided (hex) tubing fitting to provide the most grip without damage to the fitting.

Figure 2–13 Box-end wrench. Recommended to loosen or tighten a bolt or nut where a socket will not fit. A box-end wrench has a different size at each end and is better to use than an open-end wrench because it touches the bolt or nut around the entire head instead of at just two places.

Figure 2–14 Open-end wrench. Each end has a different-sized opening and is recommended for general usage. Do not attempt to loosen or tighten bolts or nuts from or to full torque with an open-end wrench because it could round the flats of the fastener.

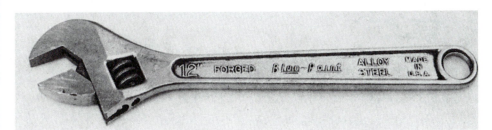

Figure 2–15 Adjustable wrench. The size (12 inches) is the *length* of the wrench, not how far the jaws open!

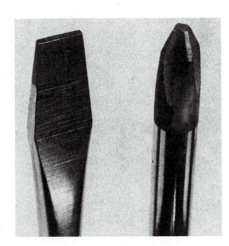

Figure 2–16 A flat-blade (or straight-blade) screwdriver (on the left) is specified by the length of the screwdriver and width of the blade. The width of the blade should match the width of the screw slot of the fastener. A Phillips-head screwdriver (on the right) is specified by the length of the handle and the size of the point at the tip. A #1 is a sharp point, #2 is most common (as shown), and a #3 Phillips is blunt and is only used for larger sizes of Phillips-head fasteners.

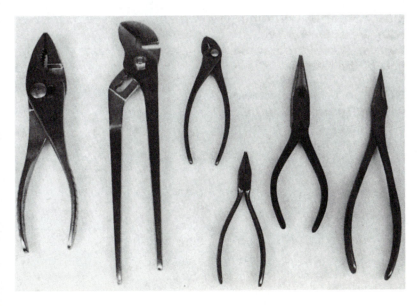

Figure 2–17 Assortment of pliers. Slip-joint pliers (far left) are often confused with water pump pliers (second from left).

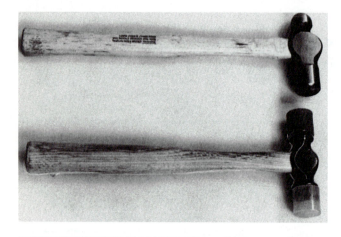

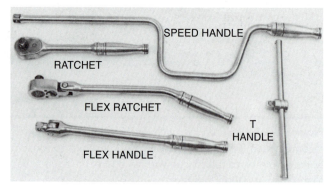

Figure 2–19 Typical drive handles for sockets.

Figure 2–18 A ball-peen hammer (top) is purchased according to weight (usually in ounces) of the head of the hammer. At bottom is a soft-faced (plastic) hammer. Always use a hammer that is softer than the material being driven. Use a block of wood or similar material between a steel hammer and steel or iron engine parts to prevent damage to the engine parts.

Figure 2–20 Various socket extensions. The universal joint (U-joint) in the center (bottom) is useful for gaining access in tight areas.

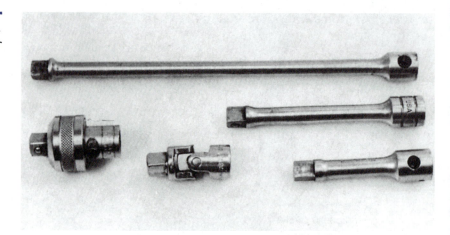

Figure 2–21 Socket drive adapters. These adapters permit the use of a ⅜-inch drive ratchet with ½-inch drive sockets, or other combinations as the various adapters permit. Adapters should *not* be used where a larger tool used with excessive force could break or damage a smaller-sized socket.

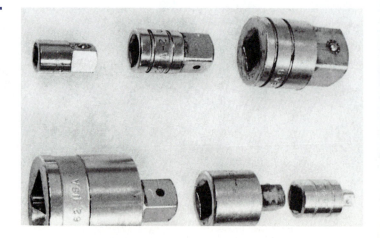

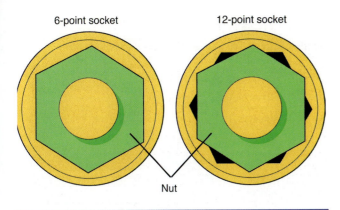

Figure 2–22 A six-point socket fits the head of the bolt or nut on all sides. A twelve-point socket can round off the head of a bolt or nut if a lot of force is applied.

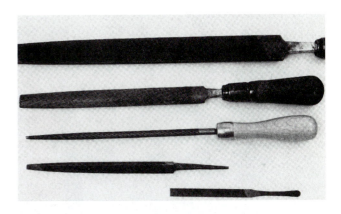

Figure 2–25 Typical files.

Figure 2–23 Standard twelve-point short socket (left), universal joint socket (center), and deep-well socket (right). Both the universal and deep well are six-point sockets.

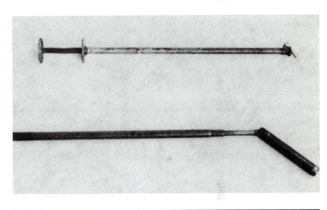

Figure 2–26 Mechanical pickup finger (top) and extendible magnet (bottom) are excellent tools to have when a nut drops down into a small area where fingers can never reach.

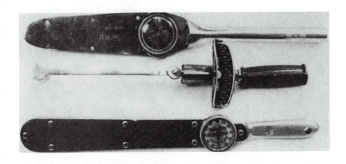

Figure 2–24 Typical torque wrenches. All of these give bolt-tightening torque in foot-pound units.

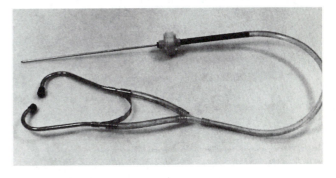

Figure 2–27 Stethoscope used by technicians to listen for the exact location of the problem noise.

Figure 2–28 Pedestal grinder with shields. This type of grinder should be bolted to the floor. A face shield should also be worn whenever using a grinder or wire wheel.

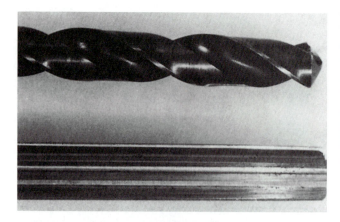

Figure 2–30 Drill bit (top) with twisted flutes (grooves) and a reamer (bottom) with straight flutes.

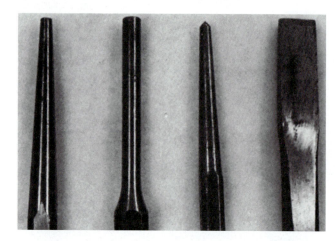

Figure 2–31 Various punches on the left and a chisel on the right.

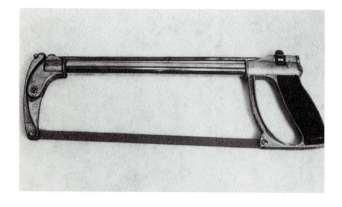

Figure 2–29 Hacksaw. The teeth of the blade should point away from the handle. The thinner the material being cut, the finer should be the blade teeth.

Figure 2–32 Using a die to cut threads on a rod.

Figure 2–33 A standard and a bottoming tap. These taps are commonly used to "chase" or clean existing threads in blocks.

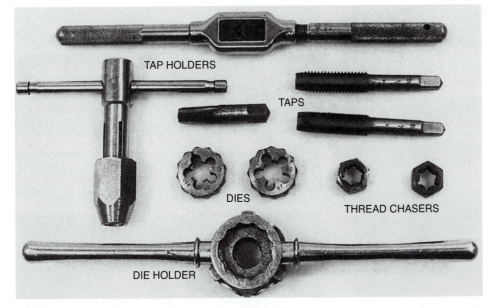

TAP HOLDERS

TAPS

DIES

THREAD CHASERS

DIE HOLDER

Figure 2–34 Dies are used to make threads on the outside of round stock. Taps are used to make threads inside holes. A thread chaser is used to clean threads without removing metal.

■ TOOL SETS AND ACCESSORIES

A beginning service technician may wish to start with a small set of tools before spending a lot of money on an expensive, extensive tool box. See Figures 2–35 through 2–37.

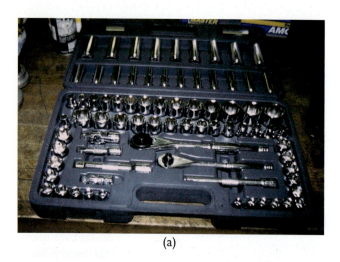

(a)

Figure 2–36 An inexpensive muffin tin can be used to keep small parts separated.

(b)

Figure 2–35 (a) A beginning technician can start with some simple basic hand tools. (b) An experienced, serious technician often spends several thousand dollars a year for tools such as found in this large (and expensive) tool box.

Figure 2–37 A good fluorescent trouble light is essential. A fluorescent light operates cooler than an incandescent light and does not pose a fire hazard, as when gasoline is accidentally dropped on an unprotected incandescent bulb used in some trouble lights.

■ BRAND NAME VERSUS PROPER TERM

Technicians often use slang or brand names of tools rather than the proper term. This results in some confusion for new technicians. Some examples are given in the following table.

Brand Name	Proper Term	Slang Name
Crescent wrench	Adjustable wrench	Monkey wrench
Vise Grips	Locking pliers	
Channel Locks	Water pump pliers or multigroove adjustable pliers	Pump pliers
	Diagonal cutting pliers	Dikes or side cuts

■ SAFETY TIPS FOR USING HAND TOOLS

The following safety tips should be kept in mind whenever you are working with hand tools:

- Always *pull* a wrench toward you for best control and safety. Never push a wrench.
- Keep wrenches and all hand tools clean to help prevent rust and for a better, firmer grip.
- Always use a 6-point socket or a box-end wrench to break loose a tight bolt or nut.
- Use a box-end wrench for torque and the open-end wrench for speed.
- Never use a pipe extension or other type of "cheater bar" on a wrench or ratchet handle. If more force is required, use a larger tool or use penetrating oil and/or heat on the frozen fastener. (If heat is used on a bolt or nut to remove it, always replace it with a new part.)
- Always use the proper tool for the job. If a specialized tool is required, use the proper tool and do not try to use another tool improperly.
- Never expose any tool to excessive heat. High temperatures can reduce the strength ("draw the temper") of metal tools.
- Never use a hammer on any wrench or socket handle unless you are using a special "staking face" wrench designed to be used with a hammer.
- Replace any tools that are damaged or worn.

■ MEASURING TOOLS

The purpose of any repair is to restore the engine or vehicle to factory specification tolerance. Every repair

procedure involves measuring. The service technician must measure twice:

- The original engine or vehicle components must be measured to see if correction is necessary to restore the component or part to factory specifications.
- The replacement parts and finished machined areas must be measured to ensure proper dimension before the engine or component is assembled or replaced on the vehicle.

Micrometer

A micrometer is the most used measuring instrument in engine service and repair. See Figure 2–38. The **thimble** rotates over the **barrel** on a screw that has 40 threads per inch. Every revolution of the thimble moves the **spindle** 0.025 inch. The thimble is graduated into 25 equally spaced lines; therefore, each line represents 0.001 inch. Every micrometer should be checked for calibration on a regular basis. See Figure 2–39. See Figure 2–40 for examples of micrometer readings.

Telescopic Gauge

A telescopic gauge is used with a micrometer to measure the inside diameter of a hole or bore.

Cylinder Bore

The cylinder bore can be measured by inserting a telescopic gauge into the bore and rotating the handle lock to allow the arms of the gauge to contact the

Figure 2–38 Typical micrometers used for dimensional inspection.

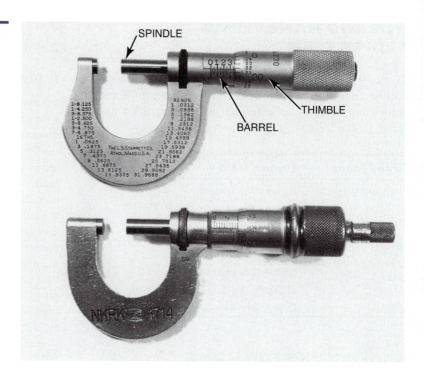

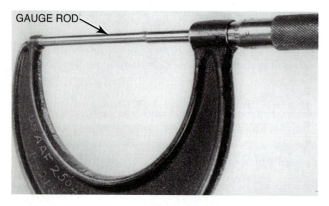

Figure 2–39 All micrometers should be checked and calibrated as needed using a gauge rod.

inside bore of the cylinder. Tighten the handle lock and remove the gauge from the cylinder. Use a micrometer to measure the telescopic gauge. See Figure 2–41. A telescopic gauge can also be used to measure the following:

- Camshaft bearing
- Main bearing bore (housing bore) measurement
- Connecting rod bore measurement

Small-Hole Gauge

A small-hole gauge (also called a **split-ball gauge**) is used with a micrometer to measure the inside diameter of small holes such as a valve guide in a cylinder head. See Figures 2–42 and 2–43.

Vernier Dial Caliper

A vernier dial caliper is normally used to measure the outside diameter or length of a component such as a piston diameter or crankshaft and camshaft bearing journal diameter. See Figure 2–44.

Feeler Gauge

A feeler gauge (also known as a thickness gauge) is an accurately manufactured strip of metal that is used to determine the gap or clearance between two

---

Frequently Asked Question   **???**

What is the Difference Between the Words *Gage* and *Gauge*?

The word *gauge* means "measurement or dimension to a standard of reference." The word *gauge* can also be spelled *gage*. Therefore, in most cases, the words mean the same.

INTERESTING NOTE: One vehicle manufacturing representative told me that *gage* was used rather than *gauge* because even though it is the second acceptable spelling of the word, it is correct and it saved the company a lot of money in printing costs because the word *gage* has one less letter! One letter multiplied by millions of vehicles with gauges on the dash and the word *gage* used in service manuals adds up to a big savings to the manufacturer.

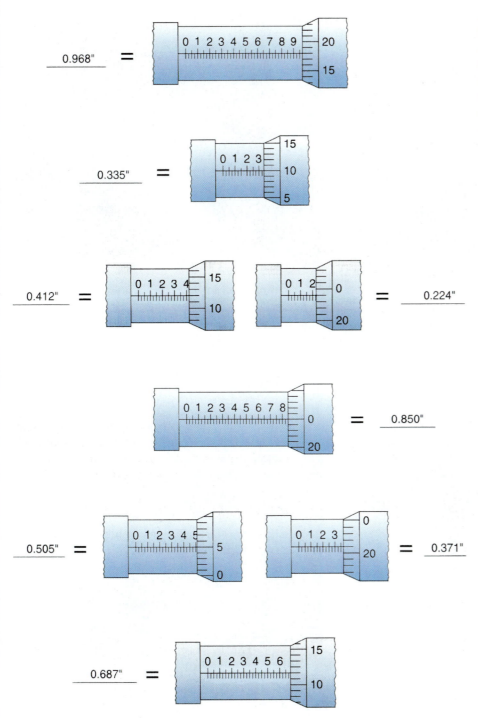

Figure 2–40 Sample micrometer readings. Each larger line on the barrel between the numbers represents 0.025″. The number on the thimble is then added to the number showing and the number of lines times 0.025″.

components. See Figure 2–45. A feeler gauge can be used to check the following:

- Piston ring gap—see Figure 2–46
- Piston ring side clearance
- Piston to cylinder wall clearance
- Connecting rod side clearance

Straightedge

A straightedge is a precision ground metal measuring gauge that is used to check the flatness of engine com-

ponents when used with a feeler gauge. A straight-edge is used to check the flatness of the following:

- Cylinder heads—see Figure 2–47
- Cylinder block deck
- Straightness of the main bearing bores (saddles)

Dial Indicator

A dial indicator is a precision measuring instrument used to measure crankshaft end play, crankshaft runout, and valve guide wear. See Figure 2–48.

(a)

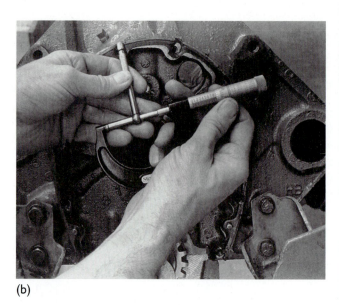
(b)

Figure 2–41 (a) A telescopic gauge being used to measure the inside diameter (ID) of a camshaft bearing. (b) An outside micrometer is used to measure the telescopic gauge.

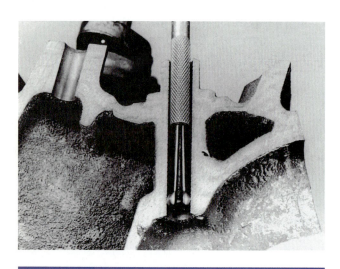

Figure 2–42 Cutaway of a valve guide with a hole gauge adjusted to the hole diameter.

Figure 2–43 The outside of a hole gauge being measured with a micrometer.

Dial Bore Gauge

A dial bore gauge is an expensive, but important, gauge used to measure cylinder taper and out-of-round as well as main bearing (block housing) bore for taper and out-of-round. See Figure 2–49. A dial bore gauge has to be adjusted to a dimension such as the factory specifications; then the reading on the dial bore gauge indicates plus (+) or minus (−) readings from the predetermined dimension. This is why a dial bore is best used to measure taper and out-of-round, because it shows the difference in cylinder or bore rather than an actual measurement.

■ SAFETY TIPS FOR TECHNICIANS

Safety is not just a buzzword on a poster in the work area. Safe work habits can reduce accidents and injuries, ease the workload, and keep employees pain free. Suggested safety tips include the following:

- *Wear safety glasses at all times while servicing any vehicle.*
- Watch your toes—always keep your toes protected with steel-toed safety shoes. If safety

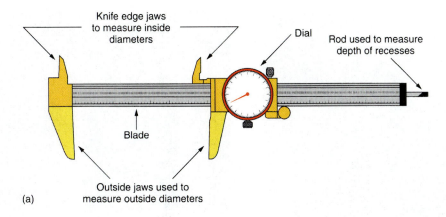

Knife edge jaws to measure inside diameters

Dial

Rod used to measure depth of recesses

Blade

(a)

Outside jaws used to measure outside diameters

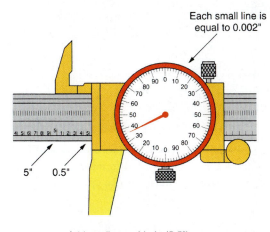

Each small line is equal to 0.002"

5"   0.5"

Add reading on blade (5.5")
to reading on dial (0.036") to
(b)   get final total measurement (5.536")

Figure 2–44 (a) A typical vernier dial caliper. This is a very useful measuring tool for automotive engine work because it is capable of measuring inside and outside measurements. (b) To read a vernier dial caliper, simply add the reading on the blade to the reading on the dial.

shoes are not available, then leather-topped shoes offer more protection than canvas or cloth.

■ Wear gloves to protect your hands from rough or sharp surfaces. Thin rubber gloves are recommended when working around automotive liquids such as engine oil, antifreeze, transmission fluid, or any other liquids that may be hazardous.

■ Service technicians working under a vehicle should wear a **bump cap** to protect the head against under-vehicle objects and the pads of the lift.

■ Remove jewelry that may get caught on something or act as a conductor to an exposed electrical circuit.

■ Avoid loose or dangling clothing.

■ When lifting any object, get a secure grip with solid footing. Keep the load close to your body to minimize the strain. Lift with your legs and arms, not your back.

■ Do not twist your body when carrying a load. Instead, pivot your feet to help prevent strain on the spine.

■ Ask for help when moving or lifting heavy objects.

■ Push a heavy object rather than pull it. (This is opposite to the way you should work with tools— never push a wrench! If you do and a bolt or nut loosens, your entire weight is used to propel your

Figure 2–45 A group of feeler gauges (also known as thickness gauges), used to measure between two parts. The long gauges on the bottom are used to measure the piston-to-cylinder wall clearance.

Figure 2–46 A feeler gauge, also called a thickness gauge, is used to measure the small clearances such as the end gap of a piston ring.

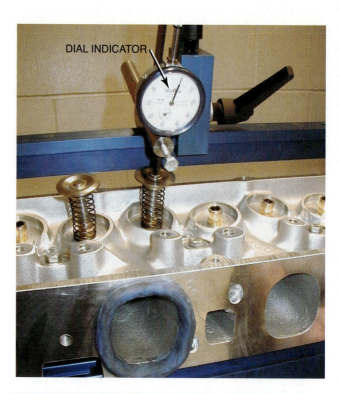

Figure 2–48 A dial indicator is used to measure valve lift during flow testing of a high performance cylinder head.

Figure 2–47 A straightedge is used with a feeler gauge to determine if a cylinder head is warped or twisted.

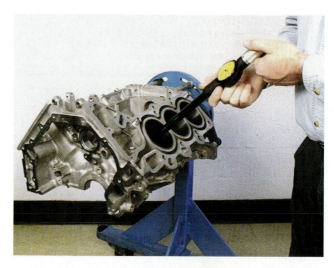

Figure 2–49 A dial bore gauge is used to check a cylinder for out-of-round and taper.

hand(s) forward. This usually results in cuts, bruises, or other painful injury.)

- Always connect an exhaust hose to the tailpipe of any running vehicle to help prevent the build-up of carbon monoxide inside a closed garage space. See Figure 2–50.
- When standing, keep objects, parts, and tools with which you are working between chest height and waist height. If seated, work at tasks that are at elbow height.
- Store all flammable liquids in an approved fire safety cabinet. See Figure 2–51.
- Always be sure the hood is securely held open. See Figure 2–52.

■ SAFETY IN LIFTING (HOISTING) A VEHICLE

Many chassis and underbody service procedures require that the vehicle be hoisted or lifted off the ground. The simplest methods involve the use of drive-on ramps or a floor jack and safety (jack) stands, whereas in-ground or surface-mounted lifts provide greater access. *Setting the pads is a critical*

Figure 2–51 Typical fireproof flammable storage cabinet.

Figure 2–50 Always connect an exhaust hose to the tailpipe of the engine of a vehicle to be run inside a building.

(a)   (b)

Figure 2–52 (a) A crude but effective method is to use locking pliers on the chrome-plated shaft of a hood strut. Locking pliers should only be used on defective struts because the jaws of the pliers can damage the strut shaft. (b) A commercially available hood clamp. This tool uses a bright orange tag to help remind the technician to remove the clamp before attempting to close the hood. The hood could be bent if force is used to close the hood with the clamp in place.

Shop Cloth Disposal

Always dispose of oily shop cloths in an enclosed container to prevent a fire. See Figure 2–53. Whenever oily cloths are thrown together on the floor or workbench, a chemical reaction can occur which can ignite the cloth even without an open flame. This process of ignition without an open flame is called spontaneous combustion.

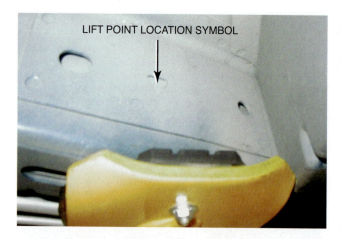

Figure 2–54 Most newer vehicles have a triangle symbol indicating the recommended hoisting lift points.

Figure 2–53 All oily shop cloths should be stored in a metal container equipped with a lid to help prevent spontaneous combustion.

part of this procedure. All automobile and light-truck service manuals include recommended locations to be used when hoisting (lifting) a vehicle. Newer vehicles have a triangle decal on the driver's door indicating the recommended lift points. The recommended standards for the lift points and lifting procedures are found in SAE Standard JRP-2184. See Figure 2–54. These recommendations typically include the following points:

1. The vehicle should be centered on the lift or hoist so as not to overload one side or put too much force either forward or rearward. See Figure 2–55.
2. The pads of the lift should be spread as far apart as possible to provide a stable platform.

3. Each pad should be placed under a portion of the vehicle that is strong and capable of supporting the weight of the vehicle.
   a. Pinch welds at the bottom edge of the body are generally considered to be strong.

CAUTION: Even though pinch weld seams are the recommended location for hoisting many vehicles with unitized bodies (unit-body), care should be taken not to place the pad(s) too far forward or rearward. Incorrect placement of the vehicle on the lift could cause the vehicle to be imbalanced, and the vehicle could fall. This is exactly what happened to the vehicle in Figure 2–56.

   b. Boxed areas of the body are the best places to position the pads on a vehicle without a frame. Be careful to note whether the arms of the lift might come into contact with other parts of the vehicle before the pad touches the intended location. Commonly damaged areas include the following:
      (1) Rocker panel moldings
      (2) Exhaust system (including catalytic converter)
      (3) Tires, especially if the edges of the pads or arms are sharp (See Figures 2–57 through 2–59.)
4. The vehicle should be raised about a foot (30 centimeters [cm]) off the floor, then stopped and shaken to check for stability. If the vehicle seems to be stable when checked at a short distance from the floor, continue raising the vehicle and continue to view the vehicle until it has reached the desired height.

(a)

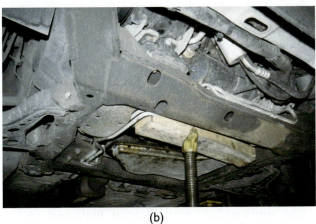

(b)

Figure 2–55 (a) Tall safety stands can be used to provide additional support for a vehicle while on a hoist. (b) A block of wood should be used to avoid the possibility of doing damage to components supported by the stand.

CAUTION: Do not look away from the vehicle while it is being raised (or lowered) on a hoist. Often one side or one end of the hoist can stop or fail, resulting in the vehicle being slanted enough to slip or fall, creating physical damage not only to the vehicle and/or hoist but also to the technician or others who may be nearby.

Figure 2–56 This vehicle fell from the hoist because the pads were not set correctly. No one was hurt, but the vehicle was a total loss.

SAFETY
ARM CLIP

Figure 2–57 The safety arm clip should be engaged to prevent the possibility that the hoist support arms can move.

HINT: Most hoists can be safely placed at any desired height. For ease while working, the area in which you are working should be at chest level. When working on brakes or suspension components, it is not necessary to work on them down near the floor or over your head; raise the hoist so that the components are at chest level.

5. Before lowering the hoist, the safety latch(es) must be released and the direction of the controls reversed. The speed downward is often adjusted to be as slow as possible for additional safety.

(a)

(b)

Figure 2–58 (a) An assortment of hoist pad adapters that are often necessary to use to safely hoist many pickup trucks, vans, and sport utility vehicles. (b) A view from underneath a Chevrolet pickup truck showing how the pad extensions are used to attach the hoist lifting pad to contact the frame.

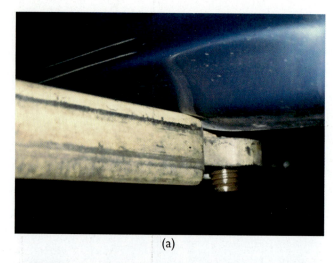

(a)

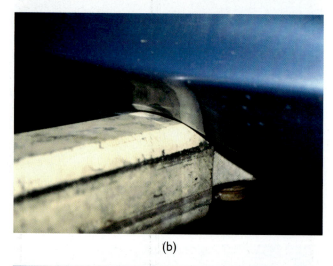

(b)

Figure 2–59 (a) In this photo the pad arm is just contacting the rocker panel of the vehicle. (b) This photo shows what can occur if the technician places the pad too far inward underneath the vehicle. The arm of the hoist has dented the rocker panel.

■ HAZARDOUS MATERIALS

The Environmental Protection Agency (EPA) regulates the handling of hazardous materials in the United States. A material is considered hazardous if it meets one or more of the following conditions:

■ It contains over 1000 parts per million (PPM) of halogenated compounds (halogenated compounds are chemicals containing chlorine, fluorine, bromine, or iodine). Common items that contain these solvents include the following:

Carburetor cleaner

Silicone spray

Aerosols

Adhesives

Stoddard solvent

Trichloromethane

Gear oils

Brake cleaner

Air-conditioning (A/C) compressor oils

Floor cleaners

Anything else that contains a chlor or
fluor in its ingredient name

- It has a flash point below 140° F (60° C).
- It is corrosive (has a pH level of 2 or lower or
12.5 or higher).
- It contains toxic metals or organic compounds.
Volatile organic compounds (VOCs) must also be
limited and controlled. This classification greatly
affects the painting and finishing aspects of the
automobile industry.

Always follow recommended procedures for the
handling of any chemicals and dispose of all used engine oil and other waste products according to local,
provincial, state, or federal laws.

To help safeguard workers and the environment,
the following guidelines are recommended:

- A technician's hands should always be washed
thoroughly after touching used engine oils,
transmission fluids, and greases. Dispose of all

waste oil according to established standards and
laws in your area. See Figure 2–60.

> **NOTE:** The Environmental Protection Agency current
> standard permits used engine oil to be recycled only if
> it contains less than 1000 parts per million of total
> halogens (chlorinated solvents). Oil containing greater
> amounts of halogens must be considered **hazardous
> waste.**

- Asbestos and products that contain asbestos are
known cancer-causing agents. Even though most
brake linings and clutch facing materials are
now manufactured without asbestos, millions of
vehicles are being serviced every day that *may*
contain asbestos. The general procedure for
handling asbestos is to put the used parts into a
sealed plastic bag and return the parts as cores
for rebuilding or dispose of them according to
current laws and regulations.
- Eyewash stations should be readily accessible
near the work area or near where solvents or
other contaminants could get into the eyes. See
Figure 2–61.

Figure 2–60 All solvents and other hazardous waste
should be disposed of properly.

Figure 2–61 An eyewash station should be centrally
located in the shop and near where solvent may be
splashed.

■ MATERIAL SAFETY DATA SHEETS

Businesses and schools in the United States are required to provide a detailed data sheet on each of the chemicals or materials to which a person may be exposed within their buildings. These sheets of information on each of the materials that *may* be harmful are called **material safety data sheets (MSDS)**. See Figure 2–62.

■ ELECTRICAL CORD SAFETY

Use correctly grounded three-prong sockets and extension cords to operate power tools. Some tools use only two-prong plugs. Make sure these are double insulated. When not in use, keep electrical cords off the floor to prevent tripping over them. Tape the cords down if they are placed in high foot traffic areas.

■ FIRE EXTINGUISHERS

There are four classes of fire extinguishers. Each class should be used on specific fires only:

- **Class A** is designed for use on general combustibles, such as cloth, paper, and wood.

- **Class B** is designed for use on flammable liquids and greases, including gasoline, oil, thinners, and solvents.
- **Class C** is used only on electrical fires.
- **Class D** is effective only on combustible metals such as powdered aluminum, sodium, or magnesium.

The class rating is clearly marked on the side of every fire extinguisher. Many extinguishers are good for multiple types of fires. See Figure 2–63.

When using a fire extinguisher, remember the word "PASS."

P = Pull the safety pin.
A = Aim the nozzle of the extinguisher at the base of the fire.
S = Squeeze the lever to actuate the extinguisher.
S = Sweep the nozzle from side to side.

See Figure 2–64.

Types of Fire Extinguishers

Types of fire extinguishers include:

- **Water**—A water fire extinguisher is usually in a pressurized container and is good to use on Class A fires by reducing the temperature to the point where a fire cannot be sustained.
- **Carbon dioxide (CO_2)**—A carbon dioxide fire extinguisher is good for almost any type of fire, especially Class B or Class C materials. A CO_2 fire extinguisher works by removing the oxygen

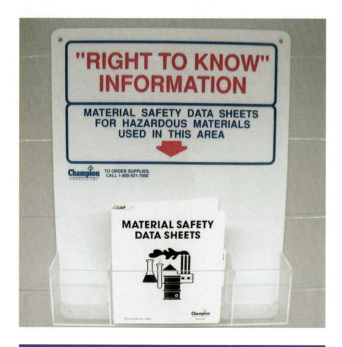

Figure 2–62 Material safety data sheets (MSDS) should be readily available for use by anyone in the area who may come into contact with hazardous materials.

| TECH TIP | |

Pound with Something Softer

If you must pound on something, be sure to use a tool that is softer than what you are about to pound on to avoid damage. Examples are given in the following table.

The Material Being Pounded	What to Pound With
Steel or cast iron	Brass or aluminum hammer or punch
Aluminum	Plastic or rawhide mallet or plastic-covered dead-blow hammer
Plastic	Rawhide mallet or plastic dead-blow hammer

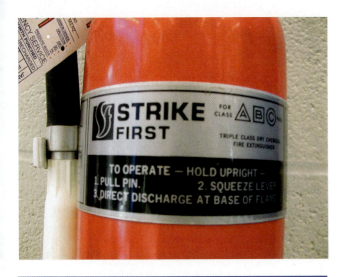

Figure 2–63 A typical fire extinguisher designed to be used on type A, B, or C fires.

Figure 2–64 A CO$_2$ fire extinguisher being used on a fire set in an open steel drum during a demonstration at a fire department training center.

from the fire, and the cold CO$_2$ also helps reduce the temperature of the fire.

■ **Dry chemical (yellow)**—A dry chemical fire extinguisher is good for Class A, B, or C fires by coating the flammable materials, which eliminates the oxygen from fire. A dry chemical fire extinguisher tends to be very corrosive and will cause damage to electronic devices.

SAFETY TIP

Air Hose Safety

Improper use of an air nozzle can cause blindness or deafness. If an air nozzle is used to dry and clean parts, make sure the air stream is directed away from anyone else in the immediate area. Coil and store air hoses when they are not in use.

P1–1 The first step in hoisting a vehicle is to properly align the vehicle in the center of the stall.

P1–2 Most vehicles will be correctly positioned when the left front tire is centered on the tire pad.

P1–3 Most pads at the end of the hoist arms can be rotated to allow for many different types of vehicle construction.

P1–4 The arms of the lifts can be retracted or extended to accommodate vehicles of many different lengths.

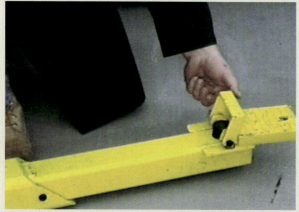

P1–5 Most lifts are equipped with short pad extensions that are often necessary to use to allow the pad to contact the frame of a vehicle without causing the arm of the lift to hit and damage parts of the body.

P1–6 Tall pad extensions can also be used to gain access to the frame of a vehicle. This position is needed to safely hoist many pickup trucks, vans, and sport utility vehicles (SUVs).

P1–7 An additional extension may be necessary to hoist a truck or van equipped with running boards to give the necessary clearance.

P1–8 Position the front hoist pads under the recommended locations as specified in the owner's manual and/or service information for the vehicle being serviced.

P1–9 Position the rear pads under the vehicle under the recommended locations.

P1–10 This photo shows an asymmetrical lift where the front arms are shorter than the rear arms. This design is best used for passenger cars and allows the driver to exit the vehicle more easily because the door can be opened wide without its hitting the vertical support column.

P1–11 After being sure all pads are correctly positioned, use the electro-mechanical controls to raise the vehicle.

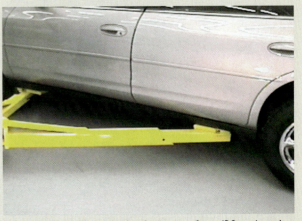

P1–12 Raise the vehicle about one foot (30 cm) and stop to double check that all pads contact the body or frame in the correct positions.

P1–13 With the vehicle raised about one foot off the ground, push down on the vehicle to check to see if it is stable on the pads. If the vehicle rocks, lower the vehicle and reset the pads. If the vehicle is stable, the vehicle can be raised to any desired working level. Be sure the safety is engaged before working on or under the vehicle.

P1–14 This photo shows the pads set flat and contacting the pinch welds of the body. This method spreads the load over the entire length of the pad and is less likely to dent or damage the pinch weld area.

P1–15 Where additional clearance is necessary for the arms to clear the rest of the body, the pads can be raised and placed under the pinch weld area as shown.

P1–16 When the service work is completed, the hoist should be raised slightly and the safety released before using the hydraulic lever to lower the vehicle.

P1–17 After lowering the vehicle, be sure all arms of the lift are moved out of the way before driving the vehicle out of the work stall.

P1–18 Carefully back the vehicle out of the stall. Notice that all of the lift arms have been neatly moved out of the way to provide clearance so that the tires will not contact the arms when the vehicle is driven out of the stall.

P2–1 This large wooden mock-up shows the use of a micrometer. The fixed part is called the barrel.

P2–2 The movable portion of the micrometer is called the thimble or sleeve.

P2–3 To read a micrometer, the numbers on the barrel represent 0.025-inch lines with numbers every 0.100 inch.

P2–4 The thimble has 25 markings that represent 0.001 inch each.

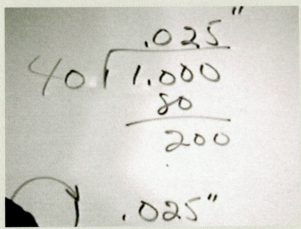

P2–5 The thimble has 40 threads per inch. Therefore, one rotation of the thimble moves it along the barrel 0.025 inch (40 into 1.000 inch equals 0.025 inch).

P2–6 To read a micrometer therefore involves both reading the lines on the barrel and adding the lines on the thimble.

Micrometer Usage—continued

P2–7 On the barrel, each rotation of the thimble is represented by one line. Each line represents 0.025 inch. Four lines represent 0.025 × 4 = 0.100 and this is marked with a "1" representing one hundred thousandth of an inch.

P2–8 This reading shows one line (0.025″) plus a zero on the thimble indicating that the thimble has rotated one complete turn beyond 0.025 inch. The second line on the barrel is barely visible. This reading is 0.050 inch.

P2–9 By rotating the thimble just one thousandth of an inch, the new reading is 0.051 inch (two lines on the barrel at 0.025 each = 0.050 plus 0.001 on the thimble = 0.051 inch).

P2–10 The thimble has been rotated enough turns so that the "1" shows on the barrel, meaning 0.100 inch (100 thousandths) plus another line indicating another 0.025 (25 thousandths) plus another 0.010 inch (10 thousandths) on the thimble. This reading is therefore 0.135 inch (100 + 25 + 10 = 135).

P2–11 This reading is 0.315 inch (0.300 on the barrel plus 0.015 inch on the thimble).

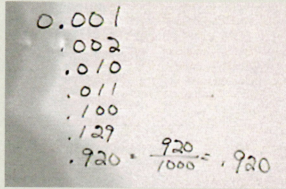

P2–12 One-thousandths of an inch is written as 0.001 inch whereas nine hundred twenty (920) thousandths of an inch is written as 0.920 inch.

SUMMARY

1. Bolts, studs, and nuts are commonly used as fasteners in the chassis. The sizes for fractional and metric threads are different and are not interchangeable. The grade is the rating of the strength of a fastener.

2. Whenever a vehicle is raised above the ground, it must be supported at a substantial section of the body or frame.

3. Hazardous materials include common automotive chemicals, liquids, and lubricants, especially those whose ingredients contain *chlor* or *fluor* in their name. Asbestos fibers should be avoided and removed according to current laws and regulations.

REVIEW QUESTIONS

1. List three precautions that must be taken whenever hoisting (lifting) a vehicle.

2. List five common automotive chemicals or products that may be considered hazardous materials.

3. List five precautions to which every technician should adhere when working with automotive products and chemicals.

4. Describe how to determine the grade of a fastener, including how the markings differ between customary and metric bolts.

ASE CERTIFICATION-TYPE QUESTIONS

1. Two technicians are discussing the hoisting of a vehicle. Technician A says to put the pads of a lift under a notch at the pinch weld of a unit-body vehicle. Technician B says to place the pads on the four corners of the frame of a full-frame vehicle. Which technician is correct?
   a. Technician A only
   b. Technician B only
   c. Both Technicians A and B
   d. Neither Technician A nor B

2. The correct location for the pads when hoisting or jacking the vehicle can often be found in the _____.
   a. Service manual
   b. Shop manual
   c. Owner's manual
   d. All of the above

3. Hazardous materials include all of the following except _____.
   a. Engine oil
   b. Asbestos
   c. Water
   d. Brake cleaner

4. To determine if a product or substance being used is hazardous, consult _____.
   a. A dictionary
   b. An MSDS
   c. SAE standards
   d. EPA guidelines

5. For the best working position, the work should be _____.
   a. At neck or head level
   b. At knee or ankle level
   c. Overhead by about 1 foot
   d. At chest or elbow level

6. When working with hand tools, always _____.
   a. Push the wrench—don't pull toward you
   b. Pull a wrench—don't push a wrench

7. A high-strength bolt is identified by _____.
   a. A UNC symbol
   b. Lines on the head
   c. Strength letter codes
   d. The coarse threads

8. A fastener that uses threads on both ends is called a _____.
   a. Cap screw
   b. Stud
   c. Machine screw
   d. Crest fastener

9. The proper term for Channel Locks is _____.
   a. Vise Grips
   b. Crescent wrench
   c. Locking pliers
   d. Multigroove adjustable pliers

10. The proper term for Vise Grips is _____.
   a. Locking pliers
   b. Slip-joint pliers
   c. Side cuts
   d. Multigroove adjustable pliers

3

Preventative Maintenance and Service Procedures

OBJECTIVES: After studying Chapter 3, the reader should be able to:

1. Prepare for ASE Engine Repair (A1) certification test content area "A" (General Engine Diagnosis) and content area "D" (Lubrication and Cooling Systems Diagnosis and Repair).
2. Correctly identify a vehicle using the vehicle identification number (VIN).
3. Perform routine fluid and service checks.
4. Describe how to install wheels and tighten lug nuts using a torque wrench and the proper sequence.
5. Describe the proper procedure for changing the engine oil and performing complete chassis system lubrication and under-vehicle inspection.

Beginning automotive service technicians are often required to perform routine service operations. It is the purpose of this chapter to introduce the reader to these various service procedures.

◼ IDENTIFYING A VEHICLE

Before service work is started, the vehicle must be properly identified to be sure that the proper replacement parts are ordered. A vehicle is first identified by make, model, and year. For example:

Make—Chevrolet
Model—Blazer
Year—1998

The year of the vehicle is often difficult to determine exactly. A model may be introduced as the next year's model as soon as January of the previous year. Typically, a new model year starts in September or October of the year prior to the actual new year, but not always. This is why the **vehicle identification number,** usually abbreviated **VIN,** is so important. See Figure 3–1. Since 1981 all vehicle manufacturers have used a VIN that is 17 characters long. Although every vehicle manufacturer assigns various letters or numbers within these seventeen characters, there are some constants, including:

- The first number or letter designates the country of origin.

1 = United States	K = Korea	
2 = Canada	L = Taiwan	
3 = Mexico	S = England	
4 = United States	V = France	
6 = Australia	W = Germany	
9 = Brazil	Y = Sweden	
J = Japan	Z = Italy	

- The model of the vehicle is commonly the fourth or fifth character.
- The eighth character is often the engine code. (Some engines cannot be determined by the VIN number.)
- The tenth character represents the year on all vehicles. See the following chart.

VIN Year Chart

A = 1980	B = 1981	C = 1982
D = 1983	E = 1984	F = 1985
G = 1986	H = 1987	J = 1988

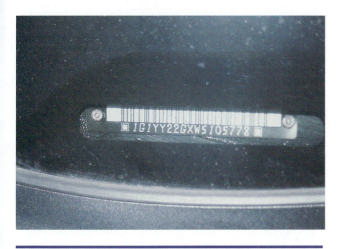

Figure 3–1 Typical vehicle identification number (VIN) as viewed through the windshield.

K = 1989	L = 1990	M = 1991
N = 1992	P = 1993	R = 1994
S = 1995	T = 1996	V = 1997
W = 1998	X = 1999	Y = 2000
1 = 2001	2 = 2002	3 = 2003
4 = 2004	5 = 2005	6 = 2006
7 = 2007	8 = 2008	9 = 2009

▉ GETTING READY FOR SERVICE

Before most service work is done, the hood (engine compartment cover) must be opened. Often the struts that hold a hood open are weak or defective. Therefore, before starting to work under the hood, always make sure that the hood is securely held open. See Figure 3–2 for two examples of how this could be done.

(a)

(b)

Figure 3–2 (a) To properly secure the hood in the open position, be certain that the prop rod is inserted into the designated opening in the hood. (b) If all else fails, the technician should use a stick or broom to hold the hood in the open position. The technician has to be careful to not bump the stick or the hood could cause serious injury.

Frequently Asked Question   ???

What Is the Julian Date?

Often, engine designs or parts change during a production year. The point at which a change occurred is usually reported to technicians in service bulletins, service manuals, or parts books as a vehicle serial number or a certain Julian date. A Julian date is simply the number of the day of the year. For example, January 1 is the day 001 and December 31 is usually day 365. The Julian date is commonly used in industry and is named for Julius Caesar, who first used a 365-day calendar, with 366 days every four years. There are calendars available that list the number of the day of the year, makes usage of the Julian date easier.

T E C H   T I P   ✔

Do No Harm

As stated in the Hippocratic oath, a doctor agrees first to do no harm to the patient during treatment. Service technicians should also try to do no harm to the vehicle while it is being serviced.

Always ask, "Am I going to do any harm if I do this?" before you do it.

To protect the fenders of the vehicle from possible damage, fender covers should always be used, as shown in Figure 3–3.

■ WIPER BLADE INSPECTION AND REPLACEMENT

Windshield wiper blades are constructed of rubber and tend to become brittle due to age. Wiper blades should be cleaned whenever the vehicle is cleaned using water and a soft cloth. Wiper blade or wiper blade insert replacement includes the following steps:

- Turn the ignition switch to on (run).
- Turn the wiper switch on and operate the wipers.
- When the wipers are located in an easy-to-reach location, turn the ignition switch off. The wipers should stop.
- Remove the insert or the entire arm as per the instructions on the replacement windshield wiper blade package.
- After double-checking that the wiper is securely attached, turn the ignition switch on (run).

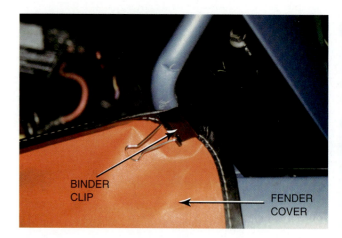

Figure 3–3 A binder clip available at most office supply stores can be used to hold a fender cover to the lip of the fender to prevent it from falling off. The clip in this photo attaches the cover to the hood hinge because this particular vehicle did not have a lip on the inside of the fender.

Figure 3–4 Installing a wiper blade insert into a wiper arm.

- Turn the wiper switch off and allow the wipers to reach the park position. Check for proper operation.

  See Figure 3–4.

■ AIR FILTER INSPECTION/REPLACEMENT

The air filter should be replaced according to vehicle manufacturer's recommendations. Many vehicle manufacturers recommend replacing the air filter every 30,000 miles (50,000 km) or more frequently under dusty conditions. Many service technicians recommend replacing the air filter every year. See Figure 3–5.

Figure 3–5 An excessively dirty air filter. This filter came from a Pontiac Bonneville that had not been serviced for over 50,000 miles!

Figure 3–6 A master brake cylinder with a transparent reservoir. The brake fluid should be between the "MAX" and the "MIN" levels as indicated on the reservoir.

■ BRAKE FLUID LEVEL INSPECTION

The brake fluid should be checked at the same time the engine oil is changed (every 3000 miles [4800 km] or every three months, whichever occurs first). There are two types of brake master cylinders:

- *Transparent Reservoir*—This type allows viewing of the brake fluid (and hydraulic clutch master cylinder if so equipped) without having to remove the cover of the reservoir. See Figure 3–6. The proper level should be between the MIN (minimum) level indicated and the MAX (maximum) level indicated on the clear plastic reservoir.
- *Metal or Nontransparent Plastic Reservoir*—This type of reservoir requires that the cover be removed to check the level of the brake fluid. The proper level of brake fluid should be 1/4" (6 mm) from the top.

> **CAUTION:** Do not overfill a brake master cylinder. The brake fluid gets hotter as the brakes are used and there must be room in the master cylinder reservoir for the brake fluid to expand.

■ BRAKE FLUID TYPES

Brake fluid is made from a combination of various types of glycol, a non-petroleum based fluid. Brake fluid is a polyalkylene-glycol-ether mixture called

polyglycol for short. *All polyglycol brake fluid is clear to amber in color.*

> **CAUTION:** DOT 3 brake fluid is a very strong solvent and can remove paint! Care is required when working with DOT 3 brake fluid to avoid contact with the vehicle's painted surfaces. It also takes the color out of leather shoes.

All automotive brake fluid must meet Federal Motor Vehicle Safety Standard 116. The Society of Automotive Engineers (SAE) and the Department of Transportation (DOT) have established brake fluid specification standards.

DOT 3

DOT 3 is the brake fluid most often used. It absorbs moisture and according to SAE, DOT 3 can absorb 2% of its volume in water per year. Moisture is absorbed by the brake fluid through microscopic seams in the brake system and around seals. Over time, the water will corrode the system and thicken the brake fluid. The moisture also can cause a spongy brake pedal action due to reduced vapor-lock temperature. See Figure 3–7. DOT 3 must be used from a sealed (capped) container. If allowed to remain open for any length of time, DOT 3 will absorb moisture from the surrounding air.

DOT 4

DOT 4 is formulated for use by all vehicles, imported or domestic. It is commonly called LMA (low

Figure 3–7 DOT 3 brake fluid. Always use brake fluid from a sealed container because the fluid absorbs moisture from the air. Such contaminated brake fluid has a lower boiling point and can cause rust to form in the brake system components.

moisture absorption) because DOT 4 does not absorb water as fast as DOT 3. It is still affected by moisture, however, and should be used only from a sealed container. The cost of DOT 4 is approximately double the cost of DOT 3. *DOT 4 can be used wherever DOT 3 is specified.*

DOT 5

DOT 5 is commonly called **silicone brake fluid** and is made from polydimethylsiloxanes. It does not absorb any water and is therefore called nonhygroscopic. DOT 5 brake fluid does not mix with and should not be used with DOT 3 or DOT 4 brake fluid.

DOT 5 brake fluid is purple (violet) in color to distinguish it from DOT 3 or DOT 4 brake fluid.

> **NOTE:** Even though DOT 5 does not normally absorb water, it is still tested using standardized SAE procedures in a humidity chamber. After a fixed amount of time, the brake fluid is measured for boiling point. Since it has had a *chance* to absorb moisture, the boiling point after this sequence is called the minimum wet boiling point.

DOT 5.1

DOT 5.1 is a non-silicone-based polyglycol fluid and is clear to amber in color. This severe duty fluid has a boiling point of over 500° F equal to the boiling point of silicone-based DOT 5 fluid. Unlike DOT 5, DOT 5.1 can be mixed with either DOT 3 or DOT 4 according to the brake fluid manufacturer's recommendations.

> **CAUTION:** Some vehicle manufacturers such as DaimlerChrysler do not recommend the use of or the mixing of other types of polyglycol brake fluid and specify the use of DOT 3 brake fluid only. Always follow the vehicle manufacturer's recommendation.

Brake Fluid Boiling Point

	Dry	Wet
DOT 3	401	284
DOT 4	446	311
DOT 5.1	500	356
DOT 5*	500	356

*Do not use DOT 5 in vehicles with ABS.

■ ENGINE OIL LEVEL AND CONDITION

The oil level should be checked when the vehicle is parked on level ground and after the engine has been off for at least several minutes. Remove the oil level indicator, commonly called a **dipstick,** wipe the oil off, and reinsert it all the way down. See Figure 3–8. Once again remove the dipstick and check where the oil level touches the indicator. The "add" mark is usually at the one quart low point. See Figure 3–9. If oil needs to be added, use the proper oil and add to the engine through the oil fill opening. Engine oil specifications and the procedure for changing the oil are included later in this chapter.

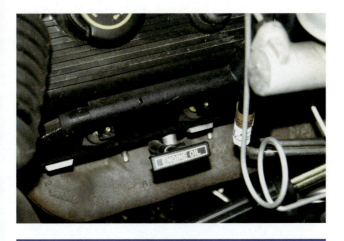

Figure 3–8 A typical engine oil level indicator (dipstick).

Figure 3–9 The oil level should read no higher than the "MAX" level and no lower than the "MIN" level when the vehicle is parked on a level surface and the oil has had some time to sit with the engine off. This time is necessary to allow the oil to flow from the upper region of the engine down into the oil pan. (Courtesy of Chrysler Corporation)

■ ENGINE OIL CHANGES

Most automotive experts recommend that the engine oil be replaced and a new oil filter installed every 3000 miles (4800 km) or every three months, whichever occurs first. Most vehicle manufacturers recommend that the oil be changed according to a "normal" or "severe use" schedule, described below.

Most vehicles are driven under severe conditions if all of these factors are considered.

■ VISCOSITY OF OIL (SAE RATING)

The word **viscosity** means resistance to flow. An oil with a high viscosity has a higher resistance to flow and is thicker than a lower-viscosity oil.

Normal Use	Severe Use
Most trips over 10 miles (16 km).	Most trips less than 4 to 10 miles (6–16 km).
Operating a vehicle when the outside temperature is above freezing (32°F/0°C).	Operating the vehicle when the outside temperature is below freezing (32°F/0°C).
Most trips do not include slow or stop-and-go driving.	Most trips include slow or stop-and-go driving.
Not towing a trailer or carrying a heavy load.	Towing a trailer or hauling a heavy load.
Driving without dusty conditions.	Driving in dusty conditions.
No police, taxi, or commercial use of the vehicle.	Use by police, taxi, or commercial operation.
The oil change interval recommended by most vehicle manufacturers under normal conditions is 7500 miles (12,000 km) or six months, whichever occurs first.	The oil change interval recommended by most vehicle manufacturers operating under severe conditions is every 3000 miles (4800 km) or every three months, whichever occurs first.

Oil is tested and assigned a viscosity number according to standards established by the Society of Automotive Engineers (SAE). It is tested at two different temperatures and assigned a number based on the oil's flow characteristics at that temperature. A thin oil is assigned a lower number and a thicker oil is assigned a higher number. Oil tested at 0° F (−18° C) has the letter W after its number. The W represents **winter.** For example, an SAE 10W engine oil was tested at 0° F and assigned a thickness rating of 10. Oil tested at 212° F (100° C) has no letter after its number. Again, the higher the number assigned, the thicker the oil. For example, an SAE 30 oil is an oil tested at 212° F.

Multi-Viscosity Engine Oils

Viscosity index (VI) improvers can be added to engine oil to prevent it from becoming thin at higher temperatures. For example, SAE 5W oil with the VI improvers added can be rated as an SAE 30 when tested at 212° F. This oil is therefore rated as an SAE 5W-30 indicating that it flowed the same as an SAE 5W when tested at 0° F and flowed the same as an SAE 30 when tested at 212° F.

Because of the wide range of temperatures at which this oil can function, multi-viscosity oils such as SAE 5W-30 and SAE 10W-30 are often the only oils recommended for use.

> **NOTE:** Some vehicle manufacturers such as Ford and Honda recommend the exclusive use of SAE 5W-20 or SAE 0W-20 engine oil. The owner's manual warns that this is the only viscosity that is acceptable to use under all temperatures and operating conditions. Always follow the vehicle manufacturer's recommended engine oil and viscosity.

■ QUALITY OF OIL (API RATING)

Although it is generally difficult to purchase low-quality oil today, it is possible to select the incorrect grade for the intended application. The quality rating is established by test procedures set up by the American Petroleum Institute (API), formerly the American Society for Testing and Materials (ASTM), with the cooperation of the Society of Automotive Engineers.

In gasoline engine oil ratings, the letter *S* means *service,* but it can be remembered as standing for oil to be used in *s*park ignition engines. The rating system is open-ended, so newer, improved ratings can be readily added as necessary (skipping the letter *I* to avoid confusion with the number 1).

Figure 3–10 API doughnut for an SAE 5W-30, SL engine oil. When compared to a reference oil, the "energy conserving" designation indicates better fuel economy.

SA	Straight mineral oil (no additives), not suitable for use in any engine
SB	Nondetergent oil with additives to control wear and oil oxidation
SC	Obsolete (1964)
SD	Obsolete (1968)
SE	Obsolete (1972)
SF	Obsolete (1980)
SG	Obsolete (1988)
SH	Obsolete (1993)
SJ	Obsolete (1997)
SL	Highest rating starting in 2001

See Figure 3–10.

> **NOTE:** Older-model vehicles for which older, now obsolete ratings were specified can use the newer, higher-rated engine oil. Newly overhauled antique cars or engines can also use the newer, improved oils. The new oils give all the protection of the older oils, plus additional protection.

Diesel classifications begin with the letter *C,* which stands for *commercial,* but which can also be remembered as standing for oil to be used in *c*ompression ignition or diesel engines.

■ ILSAC OIL RATING

The International Lubricant Standardization and Approval Committee (ILSAC) developed an oil rating that consolidates the SAE viscosity rating and the API quality rating. If an engine oil meets the standards, a "starburst" symbol is displayed on the front of the oil container. If the starburst is present, the vehicle owner and technician know that the oil is suitable for use in almost any gasoline engine. See Figure 3–11. The original GF-1 (gasoline fueled) rating was updated to GF-2 in 1997 and to GF-3 in 2001.

Figure 3–11 The International Lubricant Standardization and Approval Committee (ILSAC) star burst symbol. If this symbol is on the front of the container of oil, then it is acceptable for use in almost any gasoline engine.

TECH TIP

Wearing Rubber Gloves Saves Your Hands

Many technicians wear rubber gloves not only to help keep their hands clean but also to help protect their skin from the effects of dirty engine oil and other possibly hazardous materials. Several types of gloves and their characteristics include:

- **Latex surgical gloves**—These gloves are relatively inexpensive, but tend to stretch, swell, and weaken when exposed to gas, oil, or solvents.
- **Vinyl gloves**—These gloves are also inexpensive and are not affected by gas, oil, or solvents. See Figure 3–12.
- **Polyurethane gloves**—These gloves are more expensive, yet very strong. Even though these gloves are also not affected by gas, oil, or solvents, they do tend to be slippery.
- **Nitrile gloves**—These gloves are exactly like latex gloves, but are not affected by gas, oil, or solvents, yet they tend to be expensive.

Many service technicians prefer to use the vinyl-type gloves, but with an additional pair of nylon gloves worn under the vinyl. Nylon gloves look like white cotton gloves and when worn under the others help keep moisture under control. (Plastic gloves on a hot summer day can soon become wet with perspiration.) The nylon gloves provide additional protection and are washable.

Diesel Engines

Category	Status	Service
CH-4	Current	Introduced December 1, 1998. For high-speed, four-stroke engines designed to meet 1998 exhaust emission standards. Can be used in place of CD, CE, CF-4, and CG-4 oils.
CG-4	Current	Introduced in 1995. For severe duty, high-speed, four-stroke engines using fuel with less than 0.5% weight sulfur. Can be used in place of CD, CE, and CF-4 oils.
CF-4	Current	Introduced in 1990. For high-speed, four-stroke, naturally aspirated and turbocharged engines. Can be used in place of CD and CE oils.
CF-2	Current	Introduced in 1994. For severe duty, two-stroke-cycle engines. Can be used in place of CD-II oils.
CF	Current	Introduced in 1994. For off-road, indirect-injected and other diesel engines including those using fuel with over 0.5% weight sulfur. Can be used in place of CD oils.
CE	Obsolete	Introduced in 1987. For high-speed, four-stroke, naturally aspirated and turbocharged engines. Can be used in place of CC and CD oils.
CD-II	Obsolete	Introduced in 1987. For two-stroke-cycle engines.
CD	Obsolete	Introduced in 1955. For certain naturally aspirated and turbocharged engines.
CC	Obsolete	For engines introduced in 1961.
CB	Obsolete	For moderate duty engines from 1949 to 1960.
CA	Obsolete	For light duty engines (1940s and 1950s).

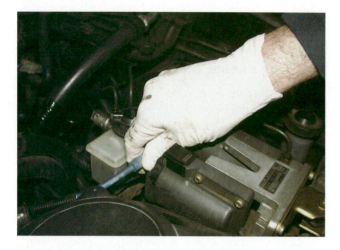

Figure 3–12 Protective gloves should be worn whenever working around grease or oil to help prevent possible skin problems. They help keep your hands clean, too!

■ SYNTHETIC ENGINE OIL

According to the Society of Automotive Engineers publications, engine oil is classified into groups as follows.

Group I—Mineral, non-synthetic, base oil with few if any additives. This type of oil is suitable for light lubricating needs and rust protection and is not to be used in an engine.

Group II—Mineral oils with quality additive packages. Most of the conventional engine oils are Group II.

Group III—Hydrogenated synthetic compounds commonly referred to as hydrowaxes. This is the lowest cost of synthetic engine oils. Castrol Syntec is a Group III oil.

Group IV—Synthetic oils made from mineral oil and monomolecular oil called polyalphaolefin or POA. Mobil 1 is an example of a Group IV synthetic oil as shown in Figure 3–13.

Group V—Non-mineral sources such as alcohol from corn called diesters or polyolesters. Red Line synthetic oil is an example of a Group V oil.

Groups III, IV, and V are all considered to be synthetic because the molecular structure of the finished product does not occur naturally and is manmade through chemical processes. All synthetic engine oils perform better than Group II (mineral) oils especially when tested according to the Noack Volatility Test ASTM D-5800. This test procedure measures the ability of an oil to stay in grade after it has been heated to 300° F (150° C) for one hour. The

Figure 3–13 Mobil 1 synthetic engine oil is used by several vehicle manufacturers in new engines.

oil is then measured for percentage of weight loss. As the lighter components boil off, the oil's viscosity will increase. If you start with an SAE 5W oil, it could test as an SAE 15W or even an SAE 20W at the end of the test. It is important that the oil you buy stay in grade for the proper lubrication of your engine.

Another major advantage of using synthetic engine oil is its ability to remain fluid at very low temperatures. This characteristic of synthetic oil makes it popular in colder climates where cold-engine cranking is important.

The major disadvantage is cost. The cost of synthetic engine oils can be four or five times the cost of Group II mineral engine oils. Some synthetic engine oils are blended with Group II mineral oils and these must be labeled as *blends*.

■ ENGINE OIL DISPOSAL

All used engine oil should be disposed of or recycled according to federal, state, provincial, or local rules and regulations. Used engine oil is considered to be

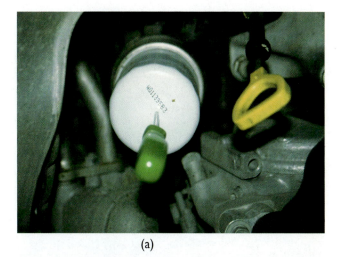

(a)

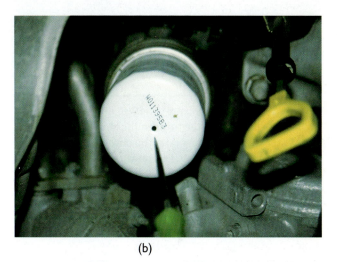

(b)

hazardous due to the dissolved metals and acids that are created in an operating engine.

■ OIL FILTERS

The oil within the engine is pumped from the oil pan through the filter before it goes into the engine lubricating system passages. The filter is made from either closely packed cloth fibers or a porous paper. Large particles are trapped by the filter, while microscopic particles will flow through the filter pores. These particles are so small that they can flow through the bearing oil film and not touch the surfaces, so they do no damage. See Figure 3–15.

Many oil filters are equipped with an **anti-drainback valve** that prevents oil from draining out of the filter when the engine is shut off. See Figure 3–16. This valve keeps oil in the filter and allows the engine to receive immediate lubrication as soon as the engine starts.

Figure 3–14 (a) A pick is pushed through the top of an oil filter that is positioned vertically. (b) When the pick is removed, a small hole allows air to get into the top of the filter which then allows the oil to drain out of the filter and back into the engine.

Either the engine or the filter has a **bypass** that will allow the oil to go around the filter element. The bypass allows the engine to be lubricated with dirty oil, rather than having no lubrication, if the filter becomes plugged. The oil also goes through the bypass when the oil is cold and thick. Most engine manufacturers recommend filter changes at every other oil change period. Correct oil filter selection includes using a filter with an internal bypass when the engine is not equipped with one.

Oil filters should be crushed and/or drained of oil before discarding. See Figure 3–17. After the oil has been drained, the filter can usually be disposed of as regular metal scrap. Always check and follow local, state, or regional oil filter disposal rules, regulations, and procedures.

OIL DRAIN-BACK VALVE

Figure 3–16 A rubber diaphragm acts as an antidrainback valve to keep the oil in the filter when the engine is stopped and the oil pressure drops to zero.

Figure 3–15 A cutaway of a typical spin-on oil filter. Engine oil enters the filter through the small holes around the center of the filter and flows through the pleated paper filtering media and out through the large hole in the center of the filter. The center metal cylinder with holes is designed to keep the paper filter from collapsing under the pressure.

Figure 3–17 A typical oil filter crusher. The hydraulic ram forces out most of the oil from the filter. The oil is trapped underneath the crusher and is recycled.

■ COOLING SYSTEM SERVICE

Normal maintenance involves an occasional check on the coolant level. The front of the radiator should be carefully inspected and cleaned of bugs, dirt, or mud that can often restrict air flow. Maintenance should also include a visual inspection for signs of coolant system leaks and for the condition of the coolant hoses and accessory drive belts.

CAUTION: The coolant level should only be checked when the engine is cool. Removing the pressure cap from a hot engine will release the cooling system pressure when the coolant temperature is above its atmospheric boiling temperature. When the cap is removed, the pressure will instantly drop to atmospheric pressure level, causing the coolant to boil immediately. Vapors from the boiling liquid will blow coolant from the system. Coolant will be lost, and a person may be injured or burned by the high-temperature coolant that is blown out of the filler opening.

The coolant-antifreeze mixture is renewed at periodic intervals. There are five types of antifreeze coolant available including:

- **Ethylene glycol**—This is the type that has been used almost exclusively since the 1950s. It is

Figure 3–18 Since the mid 1990s, many vehicle manufacturers have been using antifreeze coolant that is silicate and phosphate free. Always check the owner's manual for the specifications for the recommended engine coolant.

sweet tasting and can harm or kill animals or pets if swallowed.
- **Propylene glycol**—Similar to ethylene glycol, this type of coolant is less harmful to pets and animals because it is not sweet tasting, although it is still harmful if swallowed. This type of coolant should not be mixed with ethylene glycol coolant.

NOTE: Some vehicle manufacturers do not recommend the use of propylene glycol coolant. Check the recommendations in the owner's manual or service manual before using it in a vehicle.

- **Organic acid technology (OAT)** antifreeze coolant—This type does not contain silicates or phosphates. It is usually orange in color and was first developed by Havoline (called **DEX-COOL**) and used in General Motors vehicles starting in 1996. See Figure 3–18.
- **Hybrid organic acid technology (HOAT)**— This is a newer variation of this technology and is similar to the OAT-type antifreeze as it uses additives that are not abrasive to water pumps, yet provide the correct pH. The pH of the coolant is usually above 11. A pH of 7 is neutral, with lower numbers indicating an acidic solution and higher numbers indicating a caustic solution. If the pH is too high, the coolant can cause scaling and reduce the heat transfer ability of the coolant. If the pH is too low, the resulting acidic

Figure 3–19 Used antifreeze coolant should be kept separate and stored in a leak-proof container until it can be recycled or disposed of according to federal, state, and local laws. Note that the storage barrel is placed inside another container to catch any coolant that may spill out of the inside barrel.

solution could cause corrosion of the engine components exposed to the coolant.

- **Phosphate-free antifreeze**—Some vehicle manufacturers recommend the use of phosphate-free coolant. This coolant is ethylene-glycol based and formulated without phosphate. Some ethylene-glycol based coolant contains phosphate that could cause a white deposit to form in the cooling system if the water used to mix with the coolant is high in mineral content.

■ ANTIFREEZE/COOLANT DISPOSAL

Used coolant drained from vehicles can usually be disposed of by combining it with used engine oil. The equipment used for recycling the used engine oil can easily separate the coolant from the waste oil. Check with recycling companies authorized by local or state government for the exact method recommended for disposal in your area. See Figure 3–19.

■ RADIATOR AND HEATER HOSES

Upper and lower radiator hoses must be pliable, yet not soft. The lower hose must have a spring inside to

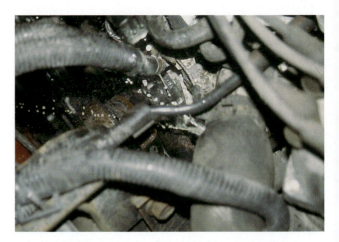

Figure 3–20 This old upper hose had a split, causing coolant to squirt out.

prevent the hose from being sucked closed, since the lower hose is attached to the suction side of the water pump. The bypass hose (if equipped) and heater hoses have a 1/2", 5/8", or 3/4" inside diameter and connect the engine cooling system to the heater core. (A heater core looks like a small radiator located inside the vehicle.) All automotive hose is constructed of rubber with reinforcing fabric weaving for strength. All hoses should be inspected for leaks (especially near hose clamps), cracks, swollen areas indicating possible broken reinforcing material, and excessively brittle, soft, and swollen sections. See Figure 3–20.

■ AUTOMATIC TRANSMISSION FLUID CHECK

The automatic transmission fluid is another vital fluid that should be checked regularly. Most automatic transmission fluid levels should be checked under the following conditions:

- The vehicle should be parked on a level surface.
- The transmission fluid should be at normal operating temperature. This may require the vehicle to be driven several miles before the level is checked.
- The engine should be running with the transmission in neutral or park as specified by the vehicle manufacturer.

NOTE: Honda and Acura manufacturers usually specify that the transmission fluid be checked with the engine off. The recommended procedure is usually stamped on the transmission dipstick or written in the owner's manual and/or service manual.

The Cut-and-Peel Trick

It is often difficult to remove a radiator or heater hose from the fittings on the radiator or heater core. To avoid possible damage to expensive radiator or heater cores, do not pull or twist the hose to remove it. Simply use a utility knife and slit the hose lengthwise and then use your finger to peel the hose off of the radiator or heater core. Although this procedure will not work if the hose is to be reused, it is a real time saver when it comes to replacing old hoses.

Quick-and-Easy Cooling System Problem Diagnosis

If overheating occurs in slow stop-and-go traffic, the usual cause is low airflow through the radiator. Check for airflow blockages or cooling fan malfunction. If overheating occurs at highway speeds, the cause is usually a radiator or coolant circulation problem. Check for a restricted or clogged radiator.

To check the automatic transmission fluid, start the engine and move the gear selector to all gear positions and return to park or neutral as specified by the vehicle manufacturer. Remove the transmission/transaxle dipstick (fluid level indicator) and wipe it off using a clean cloth. Then reinsert the dipstick until fully seated. Remove the dipstick again and note the level. See Figure 3–21.

> **NOTE:** The "add" mark on most automatic transmission/transaxle dipsticks means that 1/2 quart (1/2 liter) of automatic transmission fluid needs to be added.

■ **Do not overfill any automatic transmission/transaxle.** Even if just 1/2 quart too much were added by mistake (for example, adding 1 quart when the fluid was at the "add" line instead of the correct amount of 1/2 quart) that could cause the fluid to foam. Foaming of the ATF is caused by the moving parts inside the transmission/transaxle, which stir up the fluid and introduce air into it. This foamy fluid cannot adequately lubricate or operate the hydraulic clutches that make the unit function correctly.

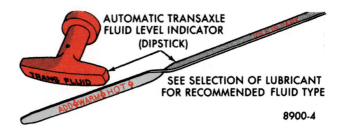

Figure 3–21 A typical automatic transmission dipstick. (Courtesy of Chrysler Corporation)

■ **Smell the ATF on the dipstick.** If it seems burned or rancid, further service of the automatic transmission/transaxle will be necessary.

■ **Look at the color of the fluid.** It should be red or light brown. A dark brown or black color indicates severe oxidation usually caused by too high an operating temperature. Further service and diagnosis of the automatic transmission/transaxle will be required. See Chapter 50.

> **NOTE:** DaimlerChrysler warns that color and smell should not be used to determine the condition of ATF+4 used in most Chrysler-built vehicles since the 2000 model year. The dyes and additives can change during normal use and it is not an indication of fluid contamination. Always follow the vehicle manufacturer's recommendation.

■ TYPES OF AUTOMATIC TRANSMISSION FLUID

Automatic transmission fluid (usually abbreviated **ATF**) is a high quality oil that has additives that resist oxidation, inhibit rust formation, and allow the fluid to flow easily at all temperatures. The automatic transmission fluid is dyed red for identification. Various vehicle manufacturers recommend a particular type of ATF based mainly on its friction characteristics. Friction is needed between the bands, plates, and clutches of an automatic transmission/transaxle. There are three types of fluid:

■ **Nonfriction modified**—This fluid does not contain any friction-reducing additives. Type F is an example of a nonfriction-modified ATF. It was primarily used in band-type Ford automatic transmissions until 1977.

■ **Friction modified**—This fluid type has additives that reduce friction. Dexron III® and Mercon V® are examples of friction-modified ATF.

TECH TIP ✔

The Paper Towel Test

New ATF will penetrate a paper towel better than used oxidized ATF. To compare old fluid with new, place three drops of new fluid on a paper towel and three drops of used ATF on the paper towel about 3 inches from the first sample. Wait for 30 minutes. The new ATF will have expanded (penetrated through the paper towel) much further than the old, oxidized fluid. This test can be used to convince a customer that the ATF should be changed according to the vehicle manufacturer's recommended interval even though, to the naked eye, the fluid looks okay.

NOTE: Mercon replaced earlier Ford ATF specifications for CJ, H, and MV.

- **Highly friction modified**—This fluid type has additional friction-reducing additives beyond those specified for a friction-modified ATF. Chrysler Mopar 7176, ATF+2, ATF+3, ATF+4, Honda, and Toyota specific ATF are examples of fluids that are highly friction modified. See Figure 3–22.

Always use the exact ATF recommended by the vehicle manufacturer.

■ POWER STEERING FLUID

The correct power steering fluid is *critical* to the operation and service life of the power steering system! The *exact* power steering fluid to use varies by vehicle manufacturer and sometimes between models made by the same vehicle manufacturer because of differences among various steering component manufacturers. See Figure 3–23.

NOTE: Remember, multiple-purpose power steering fluid does not mean *all*-purpose power steering fluid. Always consult the power steering reservoir cap, service manual, or owner's manual for the exact fluid to be used in the vehicle being serviced.

■ WINDSHIELD WASHER FLUID

Windshield washer fluid level should be checked regularly and refilled as necessary. Use only the fluid that is recommended for use in vehicle windshield washer systems. See Figure 3–24. Most windshield washer fluid usually looks like blue water. It

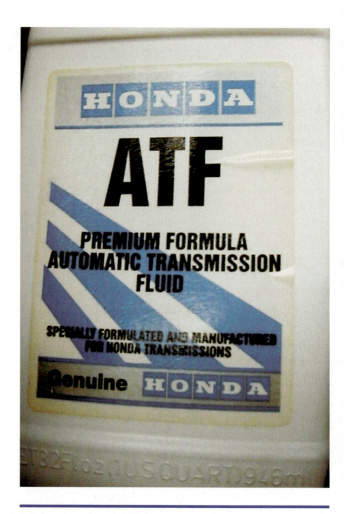

Figure 3–22 Honda ATF is highly friction modified and should be used in all Honda vehicles. Substituting another type of ATF can cause harsh shifting or shudders during acceleration.

Figure 3–23 Many vehicles use a combination filler cap and level indicator (dip stick) that shows the amount of power steering fluid in the reservoir. The power steering fluid should also be checked for color that could indicate wear in the system or contamination.

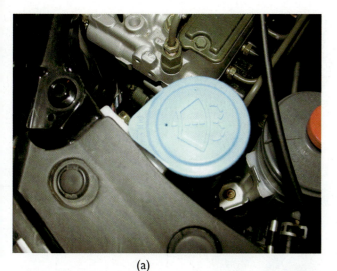

(a)

(b)

Figure 3–24 (a) Windshield washer fluid caps are usually labeled with this symbol. (b) Only use the recommended windshield washer fluid. Do not use water in climates where freezing temperatures are possible or damage to the reservoir, pump, and lines could result when the water freezes and expands.

is actually water with an alcohol (methanol) additive to prevent freezing and to help clean the windshield by dissolving bugs, etc.

CAUTION: Some mixed fluids are for summer use only and do not contain antifreeze protection. Read the label carefully! Some fluids must be mixed with water because they are in concentrated form. Follow the directions on the container *exactly*. If not enough water is used, the additives in the washer fluid could damage the paint on the roof and trunk lid. Windshield washer fluid may also be flammable because it often contains alcohol. Keep the fluid away from open flames or excessive heat.

T E C H   T I P

The Hand Cleaner Trick

Lower-than-normal alternator output could be the result of a loose or slipping drive belt. All belts (V and serpentine multigroove) use an interference angle between the angle of the V's of the belt and the angle of the V's on the pulley. A belt wears this interference angle off the edges of the V of the belt. As a result, the belt may start to slip and make a squealing sound even if tensioned properly.

A common trick used to determine if the noise is belt related is to use grit-type hand cleaner or scouring powder. With the engine off, sprinkle some powder onto the pulley side of the belt. Start the engine. The excess powder will fly into the air, so get out from under the hood when the engine starts. If the belts are now quieter, you know that it was the glazed belt that made the noise.

NOTE: Often, belt noise sounds exactly like a noisy bearing. Therefore, before you start removing and replacing parts, try the hand cleaner trick.

Often, the grit from the hand cleaner will remove the glaze from the belt and the noise will not return. However, if the belt is worn or loose, the noise will return and the belt should be replaced. A fast alternative method to determine if the noise is from the belt is to spray water from a squirt bottle at the belt with the engine running. If the noise stops, the belt is the cause of the noise. The water quickly evaporates and therefore, unlike the gritty hand cleaner, water just finds the problem—it does not provide a short-term fix.

■ ACCESSORY DRIVE BELT INSPECTION

There should be a *maximum* of 1/2" of play when a belt is depressed midway between pulleys. Power steering (PS) and air conditioning (A/C) belts usually must be even tighter. The work these belts are required to perform is deceptive. For example, an air conditioning belt must transfer approximately 12 horsepower whenever the A/C is being used. This could not be accomplished with a belt which depended on tightness alone. Most V-belts (called this because of their shape) are 34 degrees at the V. The pulley they ride through is generally 36 degrees. This 2-degree difference results in a wedging action and makes power transmission possible, but it is also the reason why V-belts must be closely inspected.

It is generally recommended that all belts, including the **serpentine** (or **Poly V**) belts be replaced

Figure 3–25 A special tool is useful when installing a new accessory drive belt. The long-handled wrench fits the hole in the belt tensioner.

Figure 3–26 Typical worn serpentine accessory drive belt. A defective or worn belt can cause a variety of noises, including squealing and severe knocking similar to a main bearing knock, if glazed or loose.

every four years. The old belts should be kept in the trunk for use in an emergency. When a belt that turns the water pump breaks, the engine could rapidly overheat, causing serious engine damage, and if one belt breaks, it often causes the other belts to become tangled, causing them to break. See Figures 3–25 through 3–27.

■ CHECKING TIRE PRESSURE

Tire pressures should be checked when the tires are cold. As a vehicle is driven, the flexing of the tire and friction between the tire and the road causes an increase in temperature. As the tire heats up, the air inside the tire also increases in temperature. The increased temperature of the air increases the air pressure inside the tire. The air pressure typically increases in pressure 4 to 6 psi after the vehicle has been driven several miles. If air is then removed from the hot tire, the tire would be underinflated. The tire pressure specified is for a tire that has not been driven and is therefore cold, so the air pressure should be checked before the vehicle has been driven more than 2 miles (3 km).

NOTE: Tire pressure changes according to air temperature about 1 psi per 10° F; therefore, during a change of season the tire pressure has to be adjusted. For example, when the summer temperature of 80° F changes to 40° F in the fall, the tire pressure will drop about 4 psi (80 − 40 = 40).

Use a good-quality tire pressure gauge and push it against the tire valve stem after removing the cap. Compare the pressure reading with the specified tire

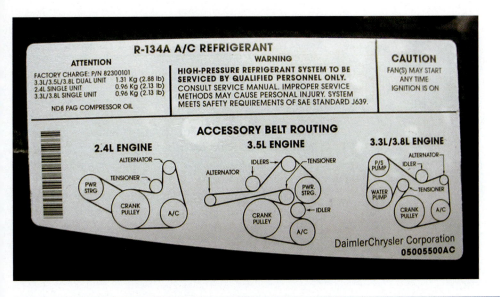

Figure 3–27 Always check the belt routing whenever replacing or checking the operation or noise in the accessory drive belts.

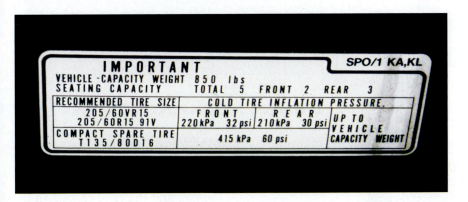

Figure 3–28 Many vehicle manufacturers print the recommended tire pressure on a placard attached to the driver's door or the door jamb.

pressure. The specified pressure is located on a placard attached to the driver's door or door post or in the glove compartment. See Figure 3–28.

> **CAUTION:** Do not inflate tires to the maximum rating on the tire sidewall. Even though this pressure represents the maximum tire pressure, inflating the tires to this pressure usually results in a very hard ride and often unacceptable handling.

The recommended tire pressure often specifies a different pressure for front and rear tires. This is very important to remember especially when the tires are being rotated. Tire pressure should be checked and adjusted if necessary after a tire rotation has been completed. The recommendation often includes a statement about tire pressures to use if operating under all highway driving conditions or

operating the vehicle in a fully loaded condition. Specifications for these conditions commonly include increasing the pressure (usually about 4 to 6 psi or 27 to 41 kPa).

■ TIRE ROTATION

To assure long life and even tire wear, it is important to rotate each tire to another location. Some rear-wheel-drive vehicles, for example, may show premature tire wear on the front tires. The wear usually starts on the outer tread row and usually appears as a front-to-back (high and low) wear pattern on individual tread blocks. These *blocks of tread* rubber are deformed during cornering, stopping, and turning, which can cause tire noise and/or tire roughness. While some shoulder wear on front tires is normal, it

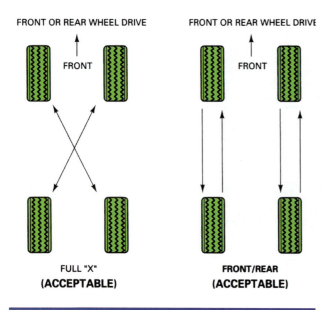

FRONT-WHEEL DRIVE

REAR-WHEEL DRIVE

FRONT

FRONT

MODIFIED "X"
(PREFERRED METHOD)

FRONT OR REAR WHEEL DRIVE

FRONT OR REAR WHEEL DRIVE

FRONT

FRONT

FULL "X"
(ACCEPTABLE)

FRONT/REAR
(ACCEPTABLE)

Figure 3–29 The preferred method most often recommended is the modified X method. Using this method, each tire eventually is used at each of the four wheel locations. An easy way to remember the sequence, whether front wheel drive or rear wheel drive, is to say to yourself, "Drive wheels straight, cross the nondrive wheels."

can be reduced by proper inflation, alignment, and tire rotation. For best results, tires should be rotated every 6000 miles or six months. See Figure 3–29 for suggested methods of rotation.

> **NOTE:** Radial tires can cause a radial pull due to their construction. If the wheel alignment is correct, attempt to correct a pull by rotating the tires front to rear or, if necessary, side to side.

Frequently Asked Question ???

"I Thought Radial Tires Couldn't Be Rotated!"

When radial tires were first introduced by American tire manufacturers in the 1970s, rotating tires side to side was *not* recommended because of concern over a belt or tread separation. Since the late 1980s, most tire manufacturers throughout the world including the United States use tire-building equipment specifically designed for radial ply tires. These newer radial tires are constructed so that the tires can now be rotated from one side of the vehicle to the other without fear of a separation being caused by the resulting reversal of the direction of rotation.

> **HINT:** To help remember when to rotate the tires, just remember that it should be done at every other oil change. Most manufacturers recommend changing the engine oil every 3000 miles (4800 km) or every three months and recommend tire rotation every 6000 (9600 km) miles or every six months.

■ WHEEL MOUNTING TORQUE

Make certain that the wheel studs are clean and dry and torqued to manufacturer's specifications. Most vehicles specify a tightening torque of between 80 and 100 lb-ft.

> **CAUTION:** Most manufacturers warn that the wheel studs should not be oiled or lubricated with grease because this can cause the wheel lug nuts to loosen while driving.

Always tighten lug nuts gradually tighter in the proper sequence (tighten one nut, skip one, and tighten the next nut). See Figure 3–30. This helps prevent warping the brake drums or rotors, or bending a wheel.

> **NOTE:** Any time you install a brand-new set of aluminum wheels, retorque the wheels after the first 25 miles. The soft aluminum often compresses slightly, loosening the torque on the wheels. See Chapter 40 for additional information on tires and wheels.

■ TIRE INSPECTION

All tires should be carefully inspected for faults in the tire itself or for signs that something may be

(a)

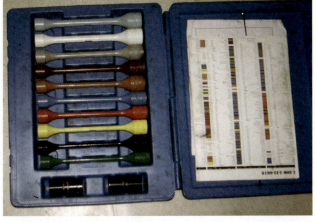

(b)

Figure 3–30 (a) A torque absorbing adapter (often called a torque stick) being used to tighten lug nuts. The adapter should not be held as it could change the torque calibration or cause personal injury if the adapter were to break. (b) An assortment of torque limiting adapters.

wrong with the steering or suspension systems of the vehicle. See Figures 3–31, 3–32, and 3–33 for examples of common problems and Chapter 40 for additional information on tire repair and tire balancing procedures.

■ CHASSIS LUBRICATION

Chassis lubrication refers to the greasing of parts that rub against each other or installing grease into

TECH TIP

Two Quick Checks

If the vehicle is hoisted on a frame-contact lift, spin each tire to check that the brakes are not dragging. You should be able to turn all four wheels by hand if the parking brake is off and the transmission is in neutral. Also, when spinning the tire, look over the top of the tire to check if it is round. An improperly mounted tire or a tire that is out-of-round can be detected by watching for the outside of the tire to move up and down as it is being rotated.

DIAGNOSTIC STORY

Waiting for the Second Click Story

A student service technician was observed applying a lot of force to a torque wrench attached to a wheel lug nut. When the instructor asked what he was doing, the student replied that he was turning the lug nut tighter until he heard a second click from the torque wrench.

This was confusing to the instructor until the student explained that he had heard a second click of the torque wrench during the demonstration. The instructor at once realized that the student had heard a click when the proper torque was achieved, plus another click when the force on the torque wrench was released.

No harm occurred to the vehicle because all of the lug nuts were reinstalled and properly torqued. The instructor learned that a more complete explanation for the use of click-type torque wrenches was needed.

Figure 3–31 All tires should be checked for wear by observing the wear bars. These strips cause the tire to be bald in this area when the tire tread depth is less than 2/32".

Figure 3–32 This tire is worn on the outside. If both front tires are worn the same way, then excessive toe-in is most likely the cause. If just one tire shows this type of wear, then the camber is not correct and the vehicle should be inspected for a fault in the suspension system.

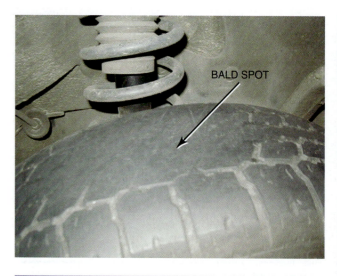

Figure 3–33 This tire should be replaced. The unusual wear pattern indicates a possible fault with the tire itself or a suspension fault that has caused the wheel/tire assembly to wear unevenly.

a pivot (or ball joints) through a grease fitting. Grease fittings are also called **Zerk fittings** (named for Oscar U. Zerk) or **Alamite fittings** (named for the manufacturer of early grease fittings). These fittings contain a one-way check valve that prevents the grease from escaping. See Figure 3–34. Grease fittings are used on steering components, such as tie-rod ends, and in the suspension ball joints, which require lubrication to prevent wear and noise caused by the action of a ball rotating within a joint during vehicle operation.

> **CAUTION:** If too much grease is forced into a sealed grease boot, the boot itself may rupture, requiring the entire joint to be replaced.

■ CHASSIS GREASE

Vehicle manufacturers specify the type and consistency of grease for each application. The technician should know what these specifications mean. Grease

is an oil with a thickening agent added to allow it to be installed in places where a liquid lubricant would not stay. Greases are named for their thickening agent, such as aluminum, barium, calcium, lithium, or sodium.

The **American Society for Testing Materials (ASTM)** specifies the consistency of grease using a **penetration test.** The **National Lubricating Grease Institute (NLGI)** uses the penetration test as a guide to assign the grease a number. Low num-

Figure 3–34 A hand-operated grease gun is being used to lubricate a grease fitting on a pitman arm.

bers are very fluid and higher numbers are more firm or hard. Most vehicle manufacturers specify NLGI #2 for wheel bearing and chassis lubrication. See Figure 3–35. NLGI also specifies grease by its use:

The "GC" designation is acceptable for wheel bearings.
The "LB" designation is acceptable for chassis lubrication.

Many greases are labeled with both GC and LB and are therefore acceptable for both wheel bearings and chassis use, such as in lubricating ball joints, tie-rod ends, etc.

■ OTHER UNDER-THE-VEHICLE LUBRICATION CHECKS

Other items underneath the vehicle that may need checking or lubricating include:

- Shock absorbers and springs (See Figure 3–36.)
- The transmission/transaxle shift linkage (check the service manual for the correct lubricant to use)
- The parking brake cable guides

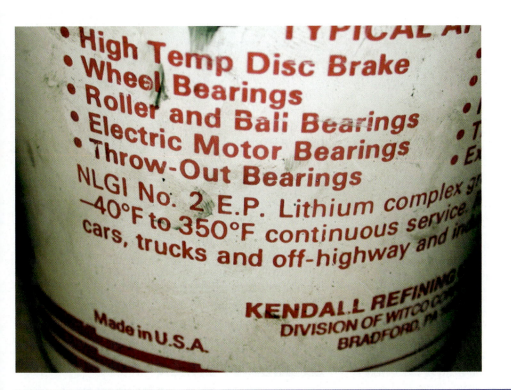

Figure 3–35 Most vehicle manufacturers recommend the use of grease rated NLGI #2 and "GC" for wheel bearings, and "LB" for chassis lubrication. Many greases have both designations and are therefore acceptable for use as wheel bearing grease as well as chassis grease for ball-joints and tie rod ends.

Figure 3–36 This broken coil spring was found during an under-vehicle inspection. The owner was unaware of the problem and it did not make any noise.

Figure 3–37 A visual inspection should include checking the differential fluid, especially after noting that a leak has occurred.

CAUTION: Do not lubricate plastic-coated parking brake cables. The lubricant can destroy the plastic coating.

■ DIFFERENTIAL FLUID CHECK

Rear-wheel drive vehicles use a differential in the rear of the vehicle to change the direction of power flow from the engine to the rear wheels. The differential also provides a gear reduction to increase engine torque applied to the drive wheels. Four-wheel drive vehicles also use a differential at the front of the vehicle in addition to the differential in the rear. To check the differential fluid level and condition, perform the following:

- Hoist the vehicle safely.
- Visually check for any signs of leakage. See Figure 3–37.
- Remove the inspection plug from the side of the differential assembly.
- Insert your small finger into the hole in the housing and then remove your finger.
  1. If the differential fluid is on your finger, then the level of the fluid is okay. Rub the fluid between your fingers. If the fluid is not gritty feeling, reinstall the inspection plug. If the fluid is gritty feeling, further service will be necessary to determine the cause and correct it. (See Chapter 47 for details.)
  2. If the differential fluid is not on your finger, then the level of the fluid is too low.

NOTE: The reason for the low fluid level should be determined. If repairs are not completed immediately, additional differential fluid should be added by pumping it into the differential through the inspection hole.

■ DIFFERENTIAL LUBRICANTS

All differentials use hypoid gear sets and a special lubricant is necessary because the gears both roll and slide between their meshed teeth. Gear lubes are specified by the **American Petroleum Institute (API).** Most differentials require:

1. SAE 80W-90 GL-5 *or*
2. SAE 75W-90 GL-5 *or*
3. SAE 80W GL-5

Limited slip differentials (often abbreviated LSD) usually use an additive that modifies the friction characteristics of the rear axle lubricant to prevent chattering while cornering.

■ MANUAL TRANSMISSION/TRANSAXLE LUBRICANT CHECK

Manual transmissions/transaxles may use any one of the following lubricants:

- Gear lube (usually SAE 80W-90)
- Automatic transmission fluid (ATF)

See Figure 3–38.

SAFETY TIP

Hand Safety

Service technicians should wash their hands with soap and water after handling engine oil or differential or transmission fluids, or wear protective rubber gloves. Another safety hint is that the service technician should not wear watches or rings or other jewelry that could come in contact with electrical or moving parts of a vehicle. See Figure 3–38.

TECH TIP

Use a Hydrocarbon Detector

One of the many items that should be inspected while underneath the vehicle is the condition of all the fuel lines. Many gasoline (fuel) leaks do not show as wet areas. A hydrocarbon detector available from automotive test equipment suppliers is an excellent tool to use to locate small gasoline leaks that may not be visible. See Figure 3–39.

Figure 3–38 Washing hands and removing jewelry are two important safety habits all service technicians should practice.

Figure 3–39 An electronic hand-held hydrocarbon tester is an excellent tool to use to check for possible gasoline leaks from lines or components.

- Engine oil (usually SAE 5W-30)
- Manual transmission fluid (sometimes called **syncromesh transmission fluid (STF)**—this type of lubricant is similar to ATF with special additives to ease shifting especially when cold)

To check manual transmissions/transaxles lubricant, perform the following:

- Hoist the vehicle safely.
- Locate the transmission/transaxle inspection (fill) plug. Consult the factory service manual for the proper plug to remove to check the fluid level.
- If the fluid drips out of the hole, then the level is correct. If the fluid runs out of the hole, the level is too full. Allow it to flow out until it stops. The correct level of fluid is at the bottom of the inspection hole.
- If low, first determine the correct fluid to use and then fill until the fluid level is at the bottom of the inspection hole or until the fluid runs out of the inspection hole.

PHOTO SEQUENCE 3   Oil Change

P3–1 Begin the oil change process by safely hoisting the vehicle.

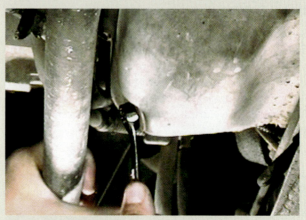

P3–2 Locate and remove the oil drain plug. On this 5.0L, V-8 Ford Mustang, two oil drain plugs are used. This is the front drain plug.

P3–3 Loosen and remove the rear oil drain plug.

P3–4 Allow the oil to drain into a suitable container. For best results, the oil drain should be close to the oil pan to help prevent the possibility of the oil splashing onto the floor or onto the service technician.

P3–5 Carefully inspect the oil drain plug and gasket. Replace the gasket as needed or specified by the vehicle manufacturer (for example, Honda specifies that the aluminum seal on the drain plug be replaced at every oil change).

Oil Change—continued

P3–6 After all of the oil has been allowed to drain from the oil pan, reinstall the plug in the rear portion of the oil pan.

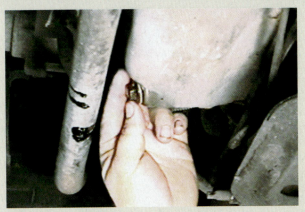

P3–7 Also replace the oil drain plug in the front portion of the oil pan.

P3–8 Using an oil filter wrench, remove the oil filter. Remember, "righty, tighty and lefty, loosy." Also be sure the oil drain pan is placed under the oil filter because oil will often drain from the filter and engine passages as the oil filter is removed.

P3–9 Check the area where the oil filter gasket seats to be sure that no part of the gasket remains that could cause an oil leak if not fully removed.

P3–10 Also check the old oil filter to make sure the gasket has been removed with the oil filter. Also compare the replacement filter with the oil filter to double check that the correct filter will be installed.

Oil Change—continued

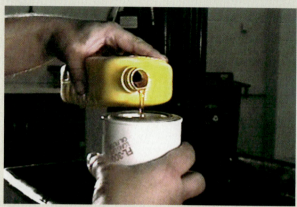

P3–11 The wise service technician adds oil to the oil filter whenever possible. This provides faster filling of the filter during start-up and a reduced amount of time that the engine does not have oil pressure.

P3–12 Apply a thin layer of clean engine oil to the gasket of the new filter. This oil film will allow the rubber gasket to slide and compress as the oil filter is being rotated on the oil filter thread.

P3–13 Install the new oil filter and tighten the recommended amount—usually 3/4 of a turn after the gasket contacts the engine.

P3–14 Use a funnel to help avoid spills and add the specified amount of oil to the engine at the oil-fill opening. Oil capacity for passenger vehicles can vary from 3 quarts (liters) to over 7 quarts (liters).

P3–15 Inspect and clean the oil-fill cap and reinstall before starting the engine.

Oil Change—continued

P3–16 Start the engine and allow it to idle while watching the oil pressure gauge and/or oil pressure warning lamp.

P3–17 The oil pressure gauge should register and the oil pressure warning lamp should go out within 15 seconds of starting the engine. If not, stop the engine and determine the cause before starting the engine again.

P3–18 Look underneath the vehicle to check for any oil leaks at the oil drain plug(s) or oil filter. Pull out the oil-level dipstick and wipe it clean with a shop cloth.

P3–19 Reinstall the oil-level dipstick to check the oil level.

P3–20 Remove the dipstick a second time and read the oil level. The oil level should be at the full mark as shown. If overfilled, hoist the vehicle and drain some oil out. An engine that has been overfilled with oil can be damaged because the oil can be aerated (filled with air like a milkshake), reducing the lubricating properties of the engine oil. Be sure to thoroughly wash your hands with soap and water after touching used engine oil or wear protective rubber gloves.

■ SUMMARY

1. The tenth character of the vehicle identification number (VIN) represents the model year of the vehicle.

2. Brake fluid should be checked regularly and not filled above 1/4" from the top of the reservoir or above the "maximum" line imprinted on the side of the master cylinder.

3. Most vehicle manufacturers specify DOT 3 brake fluid.

4. Most vehicle manufacturers specify SAE 5W-30 or 10W-30 engine oil with an API rating of SL and an ILSAC rating of GF-3.

5. The engine oil should be changed more frequently if the vehicle is driven under severe conditions such as stop-and-go city-type driving.

6. When replacing any radiator or heater hose, the end of the hose should be cut to prevent possible damage to the radiator or heater core.

7. Always use the specified automatic transmission fluid when topping off or when changing the fluid. Using the wrong type of ATF can cause the transmission to shift too harshly or cause a vibration when the transmission shifts.

8. The tire pressure should be checked when the tires are cold, and the tires should be inflated to the pressure specified on the door placard or in the owner's manual.

9. Tires should be rotated every 5000–7000 miles (8000–11,000 km) or at every other oil change.

10. Wheels should always be tightened with a torque wrench to the proper torque and in a star pattern.

11. All grease fittings should be cleaned before using a grease gun to lubricate any greaseable joints under the vehicle.

12. Most differentials require an SAE 80W-90 GL-5 rated lubricant.

13. Manual transmissions/transaxles may require one of several different lubricants including gear lube such as SAE 80W-90, ATF, engine oil (SAE 5W-30), or special manual transmission fluid.

■ REVIEW QUESTIONS

1. Explain why brake fluid should not be filled above the full or MAX level as indicated on the master cylinder reservoir.

2. Explain why brake fluid should be kept in an airtight container.

3. Explain the terms SAE 5W-30, API SL, and GF-3.

4. List three types of automatic transmission fluid.

5. Describe the most common sequence for tire rotation.

6. Discuss how to check differential fluid.

7. List four lubricants that a manual transmission/transaxle *may* require depending on exact year, make, and model of vehicle.

■ ASE CERTIFICATION-TYPE QUESTIONS

1. The model year of the vehicle is indicated in the vehicle identification number (VIN) by which character?
   a. 4th
   b. 5th
   c. 8th
   d. 10th

2. Most vehicle manufacturers specify brake fluid that meets what specification?
   a. DOT 2
   b. DOT 3
   c. DOT 4
   d. DOT 5

3. The thicker the engine oil, the better the quality.
   a. True
   b. False

4. The letter *W* as in SAE 10W-30 means
   a. Weight
   b. Wrought
   c. With
   d. Winter

5. Most antifreeze coolant is
   a. Phosphate
   b. Propylene glycol
   c. Ethylene glycol
   d. Dexthylene

6. Dexron and Mercon are examples of which type of ATF?
   a. Nonfriction modified
   b. Friction modified
   c. Highly friction modified
   d. Straight-weight mineral oil

7. Using the modified X tire rotation method on a front-wheel drive vehicle would place the right front tire on the _____.
   a. Left front
   b. Left rear
   c. Right rear

8. Most vehicle manufacturers specify a lug nut (wheel nut) tightening torque specification of about _____.
   a. 80 to 100 lb-ft
   b. 100 to 125 lb-ft
   c. 125 to 150 lb-ft
   d. 150 to 175 lb-ft

9. A grease labeled NLGI #2 GC is suitable for use on what vehicle components?
   a. Wheel bearings
   b. Chassis parts
   c. Both wheel bearings and chassis parts
   d. Door hinges only

10. A service technician removed the inspection/fill plug from the differential of a rear-wheel drive vehicle and gear lube started to flow out. Technician A says that the technician should quickly replace the plug to prevent any more loss of gear lube. Technician B says to catch the fluid and allow the fluid to continue to drain. Which technician is correct?
    a. Technician A only
    b. Technician B only
    c. Both Technicians A and B
    d. Neither Technician A nor B

Engine Repair

Chapter 4 covers basic engine operation, parts, and specifications. Chapter 5 includes all areas of engine condition diagnosis. Chapter 6 describes proper disassembly, cleaning, and crack detection procedures. Chapter 7 explains the entire cooling and engine lubrication system including problem diagnosis and service procedures. Chapter 8 covers all areas of cylinder head and valve service and Chapter 9 describes camshafts and valve train problem diagnosis and service procedures. Chapter 10 includes details on piston rings and connecting rods and Chapter 11 describes the principles and service procedures for the engine block, crankshafts, and bearings. Chapter 12 completes the section by detailing proper engine assembly and reinstallation into the vehicle.

Engine Operation, Parts, and Specifications

OBJECTIVES: After studying Chapter 4, the reader should be able to:

1. Prepare for ASE Engine Repair (A1) certification test content area "A" (General Engine Diagnosis).
2. Explain how a four-stroke cycle gasoline engine operates.
3. List the various characteristics by which vehicle engines are classified.
4. Describe how engine power is measured and calculated.
5. Discuss how a compression ratio is calculated.
6. Explain how engine size is determined.
7. Describe how turbocharging or supercharging increases engine power.

NOTE: An **external combustion engine** is an engine that burns fuel outside of the engine itself, such as a steam engine.

Engines used in automobiles are internal combustion heat engines. They convert the chemical energy of the gasoline into heat within a power chamber that is called a **combustion chamber.** Heat energy released in the combustion chamber raises the temperature of the combustion gases within the chamber. The increase in gas temperature causes the pressure of the gases to increase. The pressure developed within the combustion chamber is applied to the head of a piston or to a turbine wheel to produce a usable **mechanical force,** which is then converted into useful **mechanical power.**

■ FOUR-STROKE CYCLE OPERATION

Most automotive engines use the four-stroke cycle of events, begun by the starter motor which rotates the engine. The four-stroke cycle is repeated for each cylinder of the engine. See Figure 4–1.

■ **Intake stroke**—The **intake valve** is open and the piston inside the cylinder travels downward, drawing a mixture of air and fuel into the cylinder.

■ **Compression stroke**—As the engine continues to rotate, the intake valve closes and the piston moves upward in the cylinder, compressing the air–fuel mixture.

The engine converts part of the fuel energy to useful power. This power is used to move the vehicle.

■ ENERGY AND POWER

Energy is used to produce power. The chemical energy in fuel is converted to heat by the burning of the fuel at a controlled rate. This process is called **combustion.** If engine combustion occurs within the power chamber, the engine is called an **internal combustion engine.**

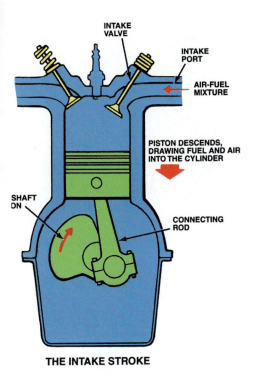

THE INTAKE STROKE

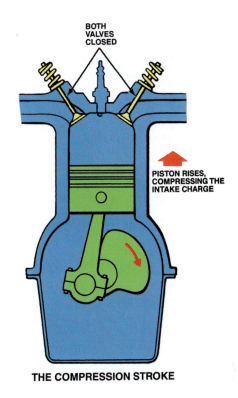

THE COMPRESSION STROKE

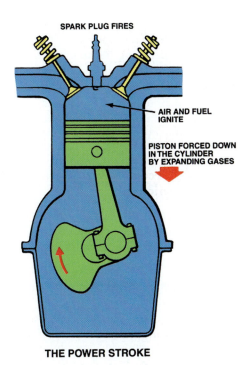

THE POWER STROKE

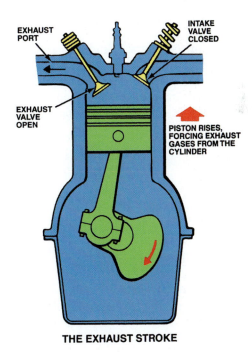

THE EXHAUST STROKE

Figure 4–1 The downward movement of the piston draws the air–fuel mixture into the cylinder through the intake valve on the intake stroke. On the compression stroke, the mixture is compressed by the upward movement of the piston with both valves closed. Ignition occurs at the beginning of the power stroke, and combustion drives the piston downward to produce power. On the exhaust stroke, the upward-moving piston forces the burned gases out the open exhaust valve.

■ **Power stroke**—When the piston gets near the top of the cylinder (called **top dead center [TDC]**), the spark at the spark plug ignites the air–fuel mixture, which forces the piston downward.

■ **Exhaust stroke**—The engine continues to rotate, and the piston again moves upward in the cylinder. The exhaust valve opens, and the piston forces the residual burned gases out of the **exhaust valve** and into the exhaust manifold and exhaust system.

This sequence repeats as the engine rotates. To stop the engine, the electricity to the ignition system is shut off by the ignition switch.

A piston that moves up and down, or reciprocates, in a **cylinder** can be seen in this illustration. The piston is attached to a **crankshaft** with a **connecting rod.** This arrangement allows the piston to reciprocate (move up and down) in the cylinder as the crankshaft rotates. See Figure 4–2. The combustion pressure developed in the combustion chamber at the correct time will push the piston downward to rotate the crankshaft.

■ THE 720° CYCLE

Each cycle of events requires that the engine crankshaft make two complete revolutions, or 720° (360° × 2 = 720°). The greater the number of cylinders, the closer together the power strokes occur. To find the angle between cylinders of an engine, divide the number of cylinders into 720°.

$$\text{Angle with four cylinders} = \frac{720°}{4} = 180°$$

$$\text{Angle with six cylinders} = \frac{720°}{6} = 120°$$

$$\text{Angle with eight cylinders} = \frac{720°}{8} = 90°$$

This means that in a four-cylinder engine, a power stroke occurs at every 180° of the crankshaft rotation (every 1/2 rotation). A V-8 is a much smoother operating engine because a power stroke occurs twice as often (every 90° of crankshaft rotation).

Engine cycles are identified by the number of piston strokes required to complete the cycle. A **piston stroke** is a one-way piston movement between the top and bottom of the cylinder. During one stroke, the crankshaft revolves 180° (1/2 revolution). A **cycle** is a complete series of events that continually repeat. Most automobile engines use a **four-stroke cycle.**

Figure 4–2 Cutaway of a Chevrolet V-8 engine showing the overhead valves, piston, connecting rod, and crankshaft.

■ ENGINE CLASSIFICATION

Engines are classified by several characteristics including:

■ **Number of strokes.** Most automotive engines use the four-stroke cycle.

■ **Cylinder arrangement.** An engine with more cylinders is smoother operating because the power pulses produced by the power strokes are more closely spaced. An inline engine places all cylinders in a straight line. Four- , five- , and six-cylinder engines are commonly manufactured inline engines. A V-type engine, such as a V-6 or V-8, has the number of cylinders split and built into a V-shape. See Figure 4–3.

■ **Longitudinal or transverse mounting.** Engines may be mounted either parallel with the length of the vehicle (longitudinally) or crosswise (transversely). See Figures 4–4 and 4–5. The same engine may be mounted in various vehicles in either direction.

NOTE: Although it might be possible to mount an engine in different vehicles both longitudinally and transversely, the engine component parts may *not* be interchangeable. Differences can include different engine blocks and crankshafts, as well as different water pumps.

■ **Valve and camshaft number and location.** The number of valves and the number and location of camshafts are a major factor in engine operation. A typical older-model engine uses one intake valve and one exhaust valve per cylinder. Many newer engines use two intake

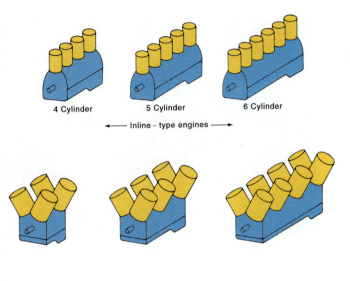

4 Cylinder　　5 Cylinder　　6 Cylinder

◄――― Inline – type engines ―――►

Figure 4–3 Automotive engine cylinder arrangements.

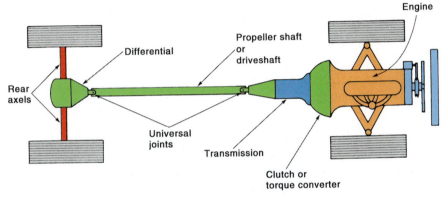

Figure 4–4 Longitudinal front engine, rear-wheel drive.

Engine

Propeller shaft
or
driveshaft

Differential

Rear
axels

Universal
joints

Transmission

Clutch or
torque converter

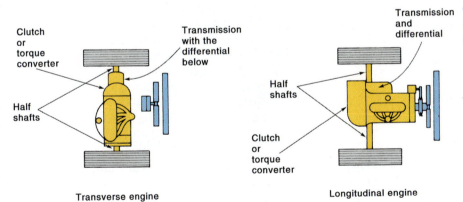

Figure 4–5 Two types of front engine, front-wheel drive.

Clutch
or
torque
converter

Transmission
with the
differential
below

Half
shafts

Transverse engine

Transmission
and
differential

Half
shafts

Clutch
or
torque
converter

Longitudinal engine

and two exhaust valves per cylinder. The valves are opened by a **camshaft.** For high-speed engine operation, the camshaft should be overhead (over the valves). Some engines use one camshaft for the intake valves and a separate camshaft for the exhaust valves. When the camshaft is located in the block, the valves are operated by lifters, push rods, and rocker arms. See Figure 4–6. This type of engine is called a **push rod engine.** An overhead camshaft engine has the camshaft above the valves in the cylinder head. When one overhead camshaft is used, the design is called a **single overhead camshaft (SOHC)** design. When two overhead camshafts are used, the design is called a **double overhead camshaft (DOHC)** design. See Figures 4–7 and 4–8.

> **NOTE:** A V-type engine uses two banks or rows of cylinders. An SOHC design therefore uses two camshafts, but only one camshaft per bank (row) of cylinders. A DOHC V-6 therefore has four camshafts, two for each bank.

Figure 4–6 Cutaway of a V-8 engine showing the lifters, push rods, roller rocker arms, and valves.

Figure 4–8 A double overhead camshaft V-6 engine with the cam covers and timing belt removed.

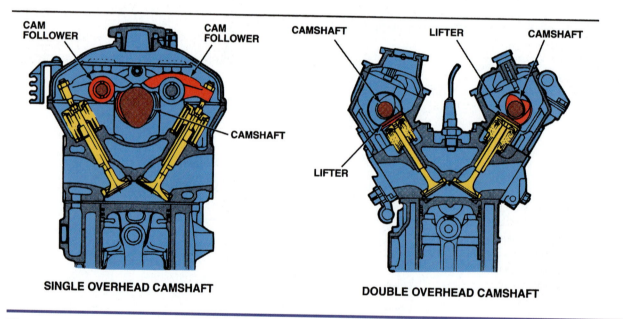

SINGLE OVERHEAD CAMSHAFT   DOUBLE OVERHEAD CAMSHAFT

Figure 4–7 Single overhead camshaft engines usually require additional components such as a rocker arm to operate all of the valves. Double overhead camshaft engines often operate the valves directly.

- **Type of fuel.** Most engines operate on gasoline, whereas some engines are designed to operate on methanol, natural gas, propane, or diesel fuel.
- **Cooling method.** Most engines are liquid cooled, but some older models were air cooled.
- **Type of induction pressure.** If atmospheric air pressure is used to force the air–fuel mixture into the cylinders, the engine is called **normally aspirated.** Some engines use a **turbocharger** or **supercharger** to force the air–fuel mixture into the cylinder for even greater power.

ENGINE ROTATION DIRECTION

The SAE standard for automotive engine rotation is counterclockwise (CCW) as viewed from the flywheel end (clockwise as viewed from the front of the engine). The flywheel end of the engine is the end to which the power is applied to drive the vehicle. This is called the **principal end** of the engine. The **nonprincipal** end of the engine is opposite the principal end and is generally referred to as the *front of*

Frequently Asked Question   **???**

What Is a Rotary Engine?

A successful alternative engine design is the **rotary engine,** also called the **Wankel engine** after its inventor. The Mazda RX-7 represents the only long-term use of the rotary engine. The rotating combustion chamber engine runs very smoothly, and it produces high power for its size and weight.

The basic rotating combustion chamber engine has a triangular-shaped rotor turning in a housing. The housing is in the shape of a geometric figure called a **two-lobed epitrochoid.** A seal on each corner, or apex, of the rotor is in constant contact with the housing, so the rotor must turn with an eccentric motion. This means that the center of the rotor moves around the center of the engine. The eccentric motion can be seen in Figure 4–9.

Figure 4–9 Disassembled Mazda rotary engine.

the engine, where the accessory belts are used. See Figure 4–10. In most rear wheel-drive vehicles, therefore, the engine is mounted longitudinally with the principal end at the rear of the engine. Most transversely mounted engines also adhere to the same standard for direction of rotation. Honda vehicles and some marine applications may differ from this standard.

■ BORE

The diameter of a cylinder is called the **bore.** The larger the bore, the greater the area on which the gases have to work. Pressure is measured in units, such as pounds per square inch (psi). The greater the area (in square inches), the higher the force exerted by the pistons to rotate the crankshaft. See Figure 4–11.

■ STROKE

The distance the piston travels down in the cylinder is called the **stroke.** The longer this distance, the greater the amount of air–fuel mixture that can be drawn into the cylinder. The more air–fuel mixture inside the cylinder, the more force will result when the mixture is ignited.

■ ENGINE DISPLACEMENT

Engine size is described as displacement. **Displacement** is the cubic inch (cu. in.) or cubic centimeter (cc) volume displaced or swept by all of the pistons. A

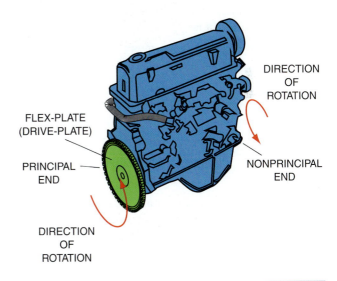

Figure 4–10 Inline four-cylinder engine showing principal and nonprincipal ends. Normal direction of rotation is clockwise (CW) as viewed from the front or accessory belt end (nonprincipal end).

liter (L) is equal to 1000 cubic centimeters; therefore, most engines today are identified by their displacement in liters.

$$1 \text{ L} = 1000 \text{ cc}$$
$$1 \text{ L} = 61 \text{ cu. in.}$$
$$1 \text{ cu. in.} = 16.4 \text{ cc}$$

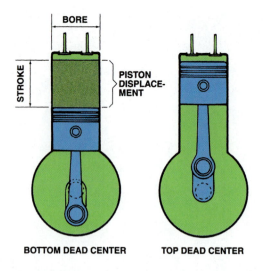

Figure 4–11 The bore and stroke of pistons are used to calculate an engine's displacement.

The formula to calculate the displacement of an engine is basically the formula for determining the volume of a cylinder multiplied by the number of cylinders. However, because the formula has been publicized in many different forms, it seems somewhat confusing. Regardless of the method used, the results will be the same. The easiest and most commonly used formula is

Bore × Bore × Stroke × 0.7854 × number of cylinders

For example, take a 6-cylinder engine where

Bore = 4.000 in., Stroke = 3.000 in.

Applying the formula,

4.000 in. × 4.000 in. × 3.000 in. × 0.7854 × 6 = 226 cu. in.

Because 1 cubic inch equals 16.4 cubic centimeters, this engine displacement equals 3706 cubic centimeters or, rounded to 3700 cubic centimeters, 3.7 liters.

Engine Size Versus Horsepower

The larger the engine, the more power the engine is capable of producing. Several sayings are often quoted about engine size:

"There is no substitute for cubic inches."

"There is no replacement for displacement."

Although a large engine generally uses more fuel, making an engine larger is often the easiest way to increase power.

Engine Size If Bored or Stroked

If an engine is bored, material is removed from the cylinder walls and a larger piston is installed. The displacement and compression ratio are both increased when the engine is bored. A stock 6-cylinder engine (like the one used in the previous displacement example) with a bore of 4.000 inches and a stroke of 3.000 inches has a displacement of 226 cubic inches. If the engine is bored to 0.060 inches oversize, the size of the bore now becomes 4.060 inches. The formula for displacement in cubic inches remains the same except that 4.060 is substituted for 4.000.

Cubic inch displacement = Bore × Bore × Stroke × 0.7854 × Number of cylinders
4.060 in. × 4.060 in. × 3.000 in. × 0.7854 × 6 = 233 cu. in. = 3818 cc.

If the bore remains the same and the stroke is increased by changing the crankshaft, the cubic inch displacement will increase and the compression ratio will also increase. If the stroke is increased 1/8 inch (0.125 in.), keeping the same stock bore, the new displacement will be calculated as follows:

Cubic inch displacement = Bore × Bore × Stroke × 0.7854 × Number of cylinders
4.000 in. × 4.000 in. × 3.125 in. × 0.7854 × 6 = 236 cu. in. = 3867 cc

If the engine is both bored and stroked (bored 0.060 inches, stroked 0.125 inches), the resultant displacement will be

4.060 in. × 4.060 in. × 3.125 in. × 0.7854 × 6 = 243 cu. in. = 3982 cc

■ COMPRESSION RATIO

The compression ratio of an engine is an important consideration when rebuilding or repairing an engine. **Compression ratio (CR)** is the ratio of the volume in the cylinder above the piston when the piston is at the bottom of the stroke to the volume in the cylinder above the piston when the piston is at the top of the stroke. See Figure 4–12.

If Compression Is Lower	If Compression Is Higher
Lower power	Higher power possible
Poorer fuel economy	Better fuel economy
Easier engine cranking	Harder to crank engine, especially when hot
More advanced ignition timing possible without spark knock (detonation)	Less ignition timing required to prevent spark knock (detonation)

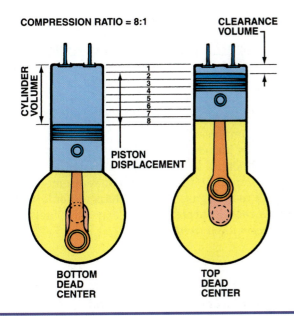

COMPRESSION RATIO = 8:1
CLEARANCE VOLUME
CYLINDER VOLUME
1 2 3 4 5 6 7 8
PISTON DISPLACEMENT
BOTTOM DEAD CENTER
TOP DEAD CENTER

Figure 4–12 Compression ratio is the ratio of the total cylinder volume (when the piston is at the bottom of its stroke) to the clearance volume (when the piston is at the top of its stroke).

TECH TIP ✔

All 3.8-Liter Engines Are Not the Same!

Most engine sizes are currently identified by displacement in liters. However, not all 3.8-liter engines are the same. See, for example, the following table:

Engine	Displacement
Chevrolet-built 3.8-L, V-6	229 cu. in.
Buick-built 3.8-L, V-6 (also called 3800 cc)	231 cu. in.
Ford-built 3.8-L, V-6	232 cu. in.

The exact conversion from liters (or cubic centimeters) to cubic inches figures to 231.9 cubic inches. However, due to rounding of exact cubic-inch displacement and rounding of the exact cubic-centimeter volume, several entirely different engines can be marketed with the exact same liter designation. To reduce confusion and reduce the possibility of ordering incorrect parts, the vehicle identification number (VIN) should be noted for the vehicle being serviced. The VIN should be visible through the windshield on all vehicles. Since 1980, the *engine* identification number or letter is usually the eighth digit or letter from the left.

Smaller, four-cylinder engines can also cause confusion because many vehicle manufacturers use engines from both overseas and domestic manufacturers. Always refer to service manual information to be assured of correct engine identification.

$$CR = \frac{\text{Volume in cylinder with piston at bottom of cylinder}}{\text{Volume in cylinder with piston at top center}}$$

For example: What is the compression ratio of an engine with 50.3-cu. in. displacement in one cylinder and a combustion chamber volume of 6.7 cu. in.?

$$CR = \frac{50.3 + 6.7 \text{ cu. in.}}{6.7 \text{ cu. in.}} = \frac{57.0}{6.7} = 8.5{:}1$$

■ COMPRESSION AFTER MACHINING

During routine engine remanufacturing, the following machining operations are performed:

1. Cylinders are bored oversize and larger-diameter pistons are installed. Boring the cylinder increases displacement and the compression ratio because the cylinder volume is increased and the combustion chamber volume remains the same, resulting in more air being squeezed into the same volume.
2. Block top surfaces are refinished. This machining operation is called *decking the block* and increases the compression ratio because it results in the cylinder heads being closer to the tops of the pistons.
3. Cylinder head(s) are resurfaced, which also increases the compression ratio.

> **NOTE:** To avoid raising the compression ratio beyond stock rating, most remanufacturers use replacement pistons that are 0.015 in. to 0.020 in. shorter than usual.

To calculate the exact compression ratio of the engine, exact measurements must be made of the bore, stroke, and combustion chamber volume. See Figure 4–13.

$$\text{Compression ratio} = \frac{(PV + DV + GV + CV)}{(DV + GV + CV)}$$

where

PV = Piston volume

DV = Deck clearance volume (volume in cylinder above piston at TDC)

GV = Head gasket volume = Bore × Bore × 0.7854 × Thickness of gasket

CV = Combustion chamber volume (if measured in cubic centimeters, divide by 16.386 to convert to cubic inches)

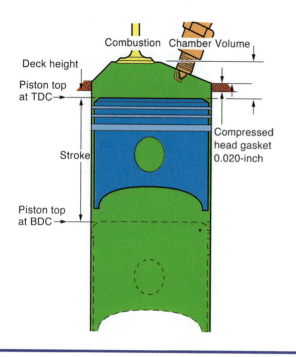

Figure 4–13 Combustion chamber volume is the volume above the piston with the piston at top dead center.

For example: What is the compression ratio of a 350-cubic inch Chevrolet V-8 if the only change made was installing 62-cc instead of 74-cc heads?

Bore = 4.000 in.

Stroke = 3.480 in.

Number of cylinders = 8

CV = 74 cc = 4.52 cu. in. and 62 cc = 3.78 cu. in.

GV = Bore × Bore × 0.7854 × Thickness of
     compressed gasket = 4.000 in. × 4.000 in. ×
     0.7854 × 0.020 in. = 0.87 cu. in.

To keep the math easier and to illustrate just the effect of changing combustion chamber volume, it is assumed that flat-top pistons are being used with zero deck-clearance volume.

> **NOTE:** This is almost never the situation but is assumed here to simplify the calculation.

$$PV = Bore \times Bore \times Stroke \times 0.7854$$
$$= 4.000 \text{ in.} \times 4.000 \text{ in.} \times 3.48 \text{ in.} \times 0.7854$$
$$= 43.73 \text{ cu. in.}$$

$$CR = \frac{(PV + DV + GV + CV)}{DV + GV + CV} = \frac{(43.73 + 0 + 0.87 + 4.52)}{0 + .87 + 4.52}$$

$$= \frac{49.12}{5.39} = 9.1:1$$

With 62-cc (3.78-cu. in.) heads,

$$CR = \frac{(PV + DV + GV + CV)}{DV + GV + CV} = \frac{(43.73 + 0 + 0.87 + 3.78)}{0 + 0.87 + 3.78}$$

$$\frac{48.38}{4.65} = 10.4:1$$

The compression ratio was increased from 9.1:1 to 10.4:1 by just changing cylinder heads from 74 cubic centimeters to 62 cubic centimeters. Because 10.4:1 compression is usually *not* recommended for use with today's gasoline, this change should only be done for racing purposes where expensive fuel or fuel additives will be used.

■ THE CRANKSHAFT DETERMINES THE STROKE

The stroke of an engine is the distance the piston travels from top dead center (TDC) to bottom dead center (BDC). This distance is determined by the throw of the crankshaft. The throw is the distance from the centerline of the crankshaft to the centerline of the crankshaft rod journal. The throw is one-half of the stroke. See Figure 4–14 for an example of a crankshaft as installed in a General Motors V-6 engine.

If the crankshaft is replaced with one with a greater stroke, the pistons will be pushed up over the height of the top of the block (deck). The solution to this problem is to install replacement pistons with the piston pin relocated higher on the piston. Another alternative is to replace the connecting rod with a shorter one to prevent the piston from traveling too far up in the cylinder. Changing the connecting rod length does *not* change the stroke of an engine. Changing the connecting rod only changes the position of the piston in the cylinder.

■ TORQUE

Torque is the term used to describe a rotating force that may or may not result in motion. Torque is measured as the amount of force multiplied by the length of the lever through which it acts. If a one-foot long wrench is used to apply 10 pounds of force to the end of the wrench to turn a bolt, then you are exerting 10 pound-feet of torque. See Figure 4–15. The metric unit for torque is Newton-meters because Newton is the metric unit for force and the distance is expressed in meters.

one pound-foot = 1.3558 Newton-meters

one Newton-meter = 0.7376 pound-foot

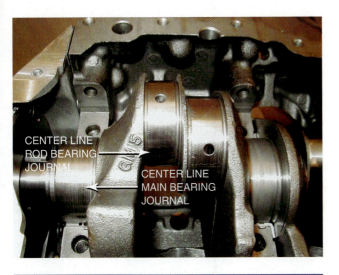

Figure 4–14 The distance between the centerline of the main bearing journal and the centerline of the connecting rod journal determines the stroke of the engine. This photo is a little unusual because this is from a V-6 with a splayed crankshaft used to even out the impulses on a 90°, V-6 engine design.

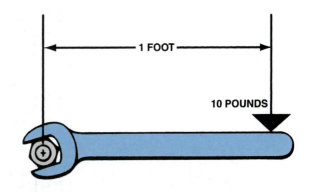

Figure 4–15 Torque is a twisting force equal to the distance from the pivot point times the force applied expressed in units called pound-feet (lb-ft) or Newton-meters (N-m).

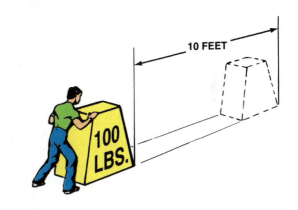

Figure 4–16 Work is calculated by multiplying force times distance. If you push 100 pounds 10 feet, you have done 1000 foot-pounds of work.

■ WORK

Work is defined as actually accomplishing movement when torque is applied to an object. A service technician can apply torque to a bolt in an attempt to loosen it, yet no work is done until the bolt actually moves. Work is calculated by multiplying the applied force (in pounds) by the distance the object moves (in feet). If you applied 100 pounds of force to move an object 10 feet, then you accomplished 1000 foot-pounds of work (100 pounds × 10 feet = 1000 foot-pounds). See Figure 4–16.

> **NOTE:** The designations for torque and work are often confusing. Torque is expressed in pound-feet because it represents a force exerted a certain distance from the object and acts as a lever. Work on the other hand is expressed in foot-pounds because work is the movement over a certain distance (feet) multiplied by the force applied (pounds). Engines produce torque and service technicians exert torque represented by the unit pound-feet.

■ POWER

The term **power** means the rate of doing work. Power equals work divided by time. Work is achieved when a certain amount of mass (weight) is moved a certain distance by a force. If the object is moved in 10 seconds or 10 minutes does not make a difference in the amount of work accomplished, but it does af-fect the amount of power needed. Power is expressed in units of foot-pounds per minute.

■ HORSEPOWER

The power an engine produces is called horsepower (hp). One **horsepower** is the power required to move 550 pounds one foot in one second, or 33,000 pounds one foot in one minute (550 lb. × 60 sec = 33,000 lb.). This is expressed as 500 foot-pounds (ft. lb.) per second or 33,000 foot-pounds per minute. See Figure 4–17.

The actual horsepower produced by an engine is measured with a **dynamometer.** A dynamometer (often abbreviated as **dyno** or **dyn**) places a load on the engine and measures the amount of twisting force the engine crankshaft places against the load. The load holds the engine speed, so it is called a **brake.** The horsepower derived from a dynamometer is called **brake horsepower (bhp).** The dynamometer actually measures the torque output of

Newton-Meters to Pound-Feet Conversion Chart
(1 N-m = 0.074 lb-ft)

N-m	Lb-ft	N-m	Lb-ft	N-m	Lb-ft	N-m	Lb-ft
1	0.74	26	19.2	51	37.7	76	56.2
2	1.5	27	20.0	52	38.5	77	57.0
3	2.2	28	20.7	53	39.2	78	57.7
4	3.0	29	21.5	54	40.0	79	58.5
5	3.7	30	22.2	55	40.7	80	59.2
6	4.4	31	22.9	56	41.4	81	59.9
7	5.2	32	23.7	57	42.2	82	60.7
8	5.9	33	24.4	58	42.9	83	61.4
9	6.7	34	25.2	59	43.7	84	62.2
10	7.4	35	25.9	60	44.4	85	62.9
11	8.1	36	26.6	61	45.1	86	63.6
12	8.9	37	27.4	62	45.9	87	64.4
13	9.6	38	28.1	63	46.6	88	65.1
14	10.4	39	28.9	64	47.4	89	65.9
15	11.1	40	29.6	65	48.1	90	66.6
16	11.8	41	30.3	66	48.8	91	67.3
17	12.6	42	31.1	67	49.6	92	68.1
18	13.3	43	31.8	68	50.3	93	68.8
19	14.1	44	32.6	69	51.0	94	69.6
20	14.8	45	33.3	70	51.8	95	70.3
21	15.5	46	34.0	71	52.5	96	71.0
22	16.3	47	34.8	72	53.3	97	71.8
23	17.0	48	35.5	73	54.0	98	72.5
24	17.8	49	36.3	74	54.8	99	73.3
25	18.5	50	37.0	75	55.5	100	74.0

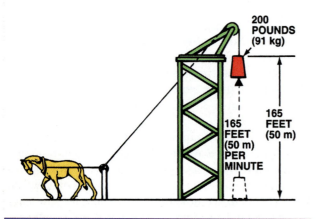

Figure 4–17 One horsepower is equal to 33,000 foot-pounds (200 lbs. × 165 ft.) of work per minute.

the engine. Torque is a rotating force that may or may not cause movement. The horsepower is calculated from the torque readings at various engine speeds (in revolutions per minute or RPM). *Horsepower is torque times RPM divided by 5252.*

$$\text{Horsepower} = \frac{\text{Torque} \times \text{RPM}}{5252}$$

Torque is what the driver "feels" as the vehicle is being accelerated. A small engine operating at a high RPM may have the same horsepower as a large engine operating at a low RPM.

Pound-Feet to Newton-Meters Conversion Chart
(1 lb-ft = 1.4 N-m)

Lb-ft	N-m	Lb-ft	N-m	Lb-ft	N-m	Lb-ft	N-m
1	1.4	26	36.4	51	71.4	76	106.4
2	2.8	27	37.8	52	72.8	77	107.8
3	4.2	28	39.2	53	74.2	78	109.2
4	5.6	29	40.6	54	75.6	79	110.6
5	7.0	30	42.0	55	77.0	80	112.0
6	8.4	31	43.4	56	78.4	81	113.4
7	9.8	32	44.8	57	79.8	82	114.8
8	11.2	33	46.2	58	81.2	83	116.2
9	12.6	34	47.6	59	82.6	84	117.6
10	14.0	35	49.0	60	84.0	85	119.0
11	15.4	36	50.4	61	85.4	86	120.4
12	16.8	37	51.8	62	86.8	87	121.8
13	18.2	38	53.2	63	88.2	88	123.2
14	19.6	39	54.6	64	89.6	89	124.6
15	21.0	40	56.0	65	91.0	90	126.0
16	22.4	41	57.4	66	92.4	91	127.4
17	23.8	42	58.8	67	93.8	92	128.8
18	25.2	43	60.2	68	95.2	93	130.2
19	26.6	44	61.6	69	96.6	94	131.6
20	28.0	45	63.0	70	98.0	95	133.0
21	29.4	46	64.4	71	99.4	96	134.4
22	30.8	47	65.8	72	100.8	97	135.8
23	32.2	48	67.2	73	102.2	98	137.2
24	33.6	49	68.6	74	103.6	99	138.6
25	35.0	50	70.0	75	105.0	100	140.0

NOTE: As can be seen by the formula for horsepower, the higher the engine speed for a given amount of torque, the greater the horsepower. Many engines are high revving. To help prevent catastrophic damage due to excessive engine speed, most manufacturers limit the maximum RPM by programming fuel injectors to shut off if the engine speed increases past a certain level. Sometimes this cutoff speed can be as low as 3000 RPM if the transmission is in neutral or park. Complaints of high-speed "miss" or "cutting out" may be normal if the engine is approaching the "rev limiter."

SAE Gross Versus Net Horsepower

SAE standards for measuring horsepower include gross and net horsepower ratings. **SAE gross horsepower** is the maximum power an engine develops without some accessories in operation. **SAE net horsepower** is the power an engine develops as installed in the vehicle. A summary of the differences is given in the following table.

SAE Gross Horsepower	SAE Net Horsepower
No air cleaner or filter	Stock air cleaner or filter
No cooling fan	Stock cooling fan
No alternator	Stock alternator
No mufflers	Stock exhaust system
No emission controls	Full emission and noise control

Ratings are about 20% lower for the net rating method. Before 1971, most manufacturers used gross horsepower rating (the higher method) for advertising purposes. After 1971, the manufacturers started advertising only SAE net-rated horsepower.

■ HORSEPOWER AND ALTITUDE

Because the density of the air is lower at high altitude, the power that a normal engine can develop is greatly reduced at high altitude. According to SAE conversion factors, a nonsupercharged or nonturbocharged engine loses about 3% of its power for every 1000 feet (300 meters [m]) of altitude.

Therefore, an engine that develops 150 brake horsepower at sea level will only produce about 85 brake horsepower at the top of Pike's Peak in Colorado at 14,110 feet (4300 meters). Supercharged and turbocharged engines are not as greatly affected by altitude as normally aspirated engines. Normally aspirated, remember, means engines that breathe air at normal atmospheric pressure.

■ TURBOCHARGING

A turbocharged (exhaust-driven) system is designed to provide a pressure greater than atmospheric pressure in the intake manifold. This increased pressure forces additional amounts of air into the combustion chamber over what would normally be forced in by atmospheric pressure. This increased charge increases engine power. The amount of "boost" (or pressure in the intake manifold) is measured in pounds per square inch (psi), in inches of mercury (in. Hg), in BAR's, or in atmospheres.

$$1 \text{ atmosphere} = 14.7 \text{ psi}$$
$$1 \text{ atmosphere} = 30 \text{ in. Hg}$$
$$1 \text{ atmosphere} = 1.0 \text{ BAR}$$
$$1 \text{ BAR} = 14.7 \text{ psi}$$

The higher the level of boost (pressure), the greater the horsepower potential. See Figure 4–18. However, other factors must be considered when increasing boost pressure:

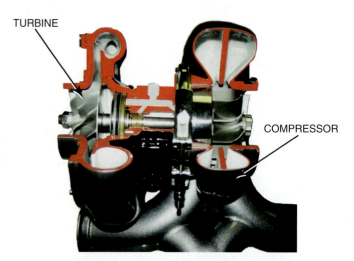

Figure 4–18 A cutaway of a typical turbocharger. The exhaust from the engine turns the turbine on the left side over 100,000 revolutions per minute. The turbine is connected by a shaft to a compressor located on the right side of the turbocharger. The compressor blades draw air from the air filter housing and force it into the intake manifold to give the engine extra power.

1. As boost pressure increases, the temperature of the air also increases.
2. As the temperature of the air increases, combustion temperatures also increase, which increases the possibility of detonation.
3. Power can be increased by cooling the compressed air after it leaves the turbocharger. *The power can be increased about 1% per 10° F by which the air is cooled.* A typical cooling device is called an **intercooler** and is similar to a radiator, wherein outside air can pass

Figure 4–19 An intercooler is a radiator-like device that is used between the turbocharger and the engine to cool the air. When air is compressed, it gets hot. Cooler air is more dense than warm air and power is increased about 1% for each 10° F drop in the temperature of air entering the engine.

Figure 4–20 Whenever the turbocharger boost pressure exceeds a predetermined value, the wastegate actuator spring compresses, which moves the wastegate valve. When the wastegate is moved, the exhaust from the engine flows directly into the exhaust system bypassing the turbocharger, which reduces the turbocharger boost pressure.

through, cooling the pressurized heated air. See Figure 4–19.

4. As boost pressure increases, combustion temperature and pressures increase, which, if not limited, can do severe engine damage. The maximum exhaust gas temperature must be 1550° F (840° C). Higher temperatures decrease the durability of the turbocharger *and* the engine.

Wastegate Operation

To prevent severe engine damage, most turbocharger systems use a wastegate. A wastegate is a valve similar to a door that can open and close. If the valve is closed, all of the exhaust travels to the turbocharger. When a predetermined amount of boost pressure develops in the intake manifold, the wastegate valve is opened. As the valve opens, most of the exhaust flows directly out the exhaust system, bypassing the turbocharger. With less exhaust flowing across the vanes of the turbocharger, the turbocharger decreases in speed and boost pressure is reduced. When the boost pressure drops, the wastegate valve closes to direct the exhaust over the turbocharger vanes and again allow the boost pressure to rise. Wastegate operation is a continuous process to control boost pressure.

The wastegate is the pressure control valve of a turbocharger system. The wastegate is usually controlled by the on-board computer. The **manifold absolute pressure (MAP) sensor** is the most important sensor used by the computer to control the

wastegate. The computer usually controls a pressure actuator, which operates the wastegate valve. See Figure 4–20.

Turbocharger Failures

When turbochargers fail to function correctly, a drop in power is noticed. To restore proper operation, the turbocharger must be rebuilt, repaired, or replaced. It is not possible to simply remove the turbocharger, seal any openings, and still maintain decent driveability. Bearing failure is a common cause of turbocharger failure, and replacement bearings are usually only available to rebuilders. Another common turbocharger problem is excessive and continuous oil consumption resulting in blue exhaust smoke. Turbochargers use small rings similar to piston rings on the shaft to prevent exhaust (combustion gases) from entering the central bearing. Because there are no seals to keep oil in, excessive oil consumption is usually caused by

1. A plugged positive crankcase ventilation (PCV) system resulting in excessive crankcase pressures forcing oil into the air inlet. This failure is not related to the turbocharger, but the turbocharger is often blamed.
2. A clogged air filter, which causes a low-pressure area in the inlet, which can draw oil past the turbo shaft rings and into the intake manifold.
3. A clogged oil return (drain) line from the turbocharger to the oil pan (sump), which can cause the engine oil pressure to force oil past the

If One Is Good, Two Are Better

A turbocharger uses the exhaust from the engine to spin a turbine, which is connected to an impeller inside a turbocharger. This impeller then forces air into the engine under pressure higher than is normally achieved without a turbocharger. The more air that can be forced into an engine, the greater the power potential. A V-type engine has two exhaust manifolds, so two turbochargers can be used to help force greater quantities of air into an engine as shown in Figure 4–21.

Boost Is the Result of Restriction

The boost pressure of a turbocharger (or supercharger) is commonly measured in pounds per square inch. If a cylinder head is restricted because of small valves and ports, the turbocharger will quickly provide boost. Boost results when the air being forced into the cylinder heads cannot flow into the cylinders fast enough and "piles up" in the intake manifold, increasing boost pressure. If an engine had large valves and ports, the turbocharger could provide a much greater *amount* of air into the engine at the same boost pressure as an identical engine with smaller valves and ports. Therefore by increasing the size of the valves, a turbocharged or supercharged engine will be capable of producing much greater power.

Figure 4–21 A dual turbocharger system installed on a small block Chevrolet V-8 engine.

Figure 4–22 A high-performance engine equipped with a belt-driven supercharger. Because a supercharger is always turning when the engine is running, a supercharger provides additional power all the time without the slight delay or lag often associated with turbocharged engines.

turbocharger's shaft rings and into the intake *and* exhaust manifolds. Obviously, oil being forced into both the intake and exhaust would create lots of smoke.

■ SUPERCHARGING

A supercharging system is an engine-driven system designed to provide pressure greater than atmospheric pressure in the intake manifold. A supercharger is used in some engines from the factory including the General Motors 3800 cc, V-6, which uses an Eaton-built unit. See Figure 4–22.

■ SUMMARY

1. The four strokes of the four-stroke cycle are intake, compression, power, and exhaust.

2. Engines are classified by number and arrangement of cylinders and by number and location of valves and camshafts, as well as by type of mounting, fuel used, cooling method, and induction pressure.

3. Most engines rotate clockwise as viewed from the front (accessory) end of the engine. The SAE standard

is counterclockwise as viewed from the principal (flywheel) end of the engine.

4. Engine size is called displacement and represents the volume displaced or swept by all of the pistons.

5. Engine power is expressed in horsepower, which is a calculated value based on the amount of torque or twisting force the engine produces.

◼ REVIEW QUESTIONS

1. Name the strokes of a four-stroke cycle.

2. What does a dynamometer actually measure?

3. What is the difference between SAE net and SAE gross horsepower?

4. If an engine at sea level produces 100 horsepower, how many horsepower would it develop at 6000 feet of altitude?

◼ ASE CERTIFICATION-TYPE QUESTIONS

1. All overhead valve engines _____.
   a. Use an overhead camshaft
   b. Have the overhead valves in the head
   c. Operate by the two-stroke cycle
   d. Use the camshaft to close the valves

2. An SOHC V-8 engine has how many camshafts?
   a. One
   b. Two
   c. Three
   d. Four

3. Brake horsepower is calculated by which of the following?
   a. Torque times RPM
   b. 2 π times stroke
   c. Torque times RPM divided by 5252
   d. Stroke times bore times 3300

4. Torque is expressed in units of _____.
   a. Pound-feet
   b. Foot-pounds
   c. Foot-pounds per minute
   d. Pound-feet per second

5. Horsepower is expressed in units of _____.
   a. Pound-feet
   b. Foot-pounds
   c. Foot-pounds per minute
   d. Pound-feet per second

6. A normally aspirated automobile engine loses about _____ power per 1000 feet of altitude.
   a. 1%
   b. 3%
   c. 5%
   d. 6%

7. One cylinder of an automotive four-stroke cycle engine completes a cycle every _____.
   a. 90°
   b. 180°
   c. 360°
   d. 720°

8. How many rotations of the crankshaft are required to complete each stroke of a four-stroke cycle engine?
   a. One-fourth
   b. One-half
   c. One
   d. Two

9. A rotating force is called _____.
   a. Horsepower
   b. Torque
   c. Combustion pressure
   d. Eccentric movement

10. Technician A says that a clogged PCV valve can cause an engine to burn oil. Technician B says that a defective turbocharger wastegate can cause the engine to burn oil. Which technician is correct?
    a. Technician A only
    b. Technician B only
    c. Both Technicians A and B
    d. Neither Technician A nor B

Engine Condition Diagnosis

OBJECTIVES: After studying Chapter 5, the reader should be able to:

1. Prepare for ASE Engine Repair (A1) certification test content area "A" (General Engine Diagnosis) and Engine Performance (A8) certification test content area "A" (General Engine Diagnosis).
2. List the visual checks that can be performed to determine the engine condition.
3. Describe how to perform a dry and wet compression test.
4. Explain how to perform a cylinder leakage test.
5. Describe how an oil sample analysis can be used to determine the engine condition.

■ ENGINE SMOKE DIAGNOSIS

The color of engine exhaust smoke can indicate what engine problem might exist.

Typical Exhaust Smoke Color	Possible Causes
Blue	Blue exhaust indicates that the engine is burning oil. Oil is getting into the combustion chamber either past the piston rings or past the valve stem seals. Blue smoke only after start-up is usually due to defective valve stem seals. See Figure 5–1.
Black	Black exhaust smoke is due to excessive fuel being burned in the combustion chamber. Typical causes include a defective or misadjusted carburetor, leaking fuel injector, or excessive fuel pump pressure.
White (steam)	White smoke or steam from the exhaust is normal during cold weather and represents condensed steam. Every engine creates about one gallon of water for each gallon of gasoline burned. If the steam from the exhaust is excessive, then water (coolant) is getting into the combustion chamber. Typical causes include a defective cylinder head gasket, a cracked cylinder head, or in severe cases, a cracked block. See Figure 5–2.

NOTE: White smoke can also be created when automatic transmission fluid (ATF) is burned. A common source of ATF getting into the engine is through a defective vacuum modulator valve on the automatic transmission. |

■ ENGINE NOISE DIAGNOSIS

An engine noise is often difficult to diagnose. Several items that can cause an engine noise include the following:

- **Valves clicking** because of lack of oil to the lifters. This noise is most noticeable at idle when the oil pressure is the lowest.
- **Torque converter** attaching bolts or nuts loose on the flex plate. This noise is most noticeable at idle or when there is no load on the engine.
- **Cracked flex plate.** The noise of a cracked flex plate is often mistaken for a rod or main bearing noise.

Figure 5–1 Blowby gases coming out of the crankcase vent hose. Excessive amounts of combustion gases flow past the piston rings and into the crankcase.

Figure 5–2 White steam is usually an indication of a blown (defective) cylinder head gasket that allows engine coolant to flow into the combustion chamber where it is turned to steam.

- **Loose or defective drive belts.** If an accessory drive belt is loose or defective, the flopping noise often sounds similar to a bearing knock.
- **Piston pin knock.** This knocking noise is usually not affected by load on the cylinder. If the clearance is too great, a double knock is heard when the engine idles. If all cylinders are grounded out one at a time and the noise does not change, a defective piston pin could be the cause.
- **Piston slap.** A piston slap is usually caused by an undersize or improperly shaped piston or oversize cylinder bore. A piston slap is most noticeable when the engine is cold and tends to decrease or stop as the piston expands during engine operation.
- **Timing chain noise.** An excessively loose timing chain can cause a severe knocking noise when the chain hits the timing chain cover. This noise often sounds like a rod bearing knock.
- **Heat riser noise.** A loose (worn) or defective heat riser valve in the exhaust on older model vehicles can make a knocking noise similar to a bearing noise. Even a vacuum-controlled heat riser (also called an **early fuel evaporation (EFE) valve**) can make a knocking noise, especially under load, as the result of slight vacuum variations applied to the actuator diaphragm. To eliminate the heat riser as a possible cause, remove the vacuum hose to the actuator or restrain the thermostatic valve with a wire or other suitable means.
- **Rod bearing noise.** The noise from a defective rod bearing is usually load sensitive and changes in intensity as the load on the engine increases and decreases. A rod bearing failure can often be detected by grounding out the spark plugs one cylinder at a time. If the knocking noise

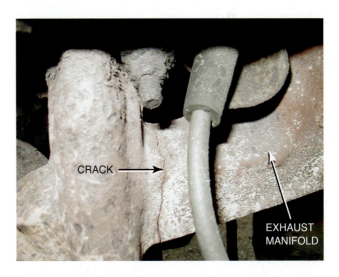

Figure 5–3 A cracked exhaust manifold on a Ford V-8.

decreases or is eliminated when a particular cylinder is grounded, then the grounded cylinder is the one from which the noise is originating.
- **Main bearing knock.** A main bearing knock often cannot be isolated to a particular cylinder. The sound can vary in intensity and may disappear at times depending on engine load.
- **Exhaust leak.** This noise may sound like a noisy valve because it often makes a clicking sound, especially during acceleration. See Figure 5–3.

Regardless of the type of loud knocking noise, after the external causes of knocking noise have been eliminated, the engine should be disassembled and carefully inspected to determine the exact cause.

Typical Noises	Possible Causes
Clicking noise (like the clicking of a ball-point pen)	**1.** Loose spark plug
	2. Loose accessory mount (for air conditioning compressor, alternator, power steering pump, etc.)
	3. Loose rocker arm
	4. Worn rocker arm pedestal
	5. Fuel pump (broken mechanical fuel pump return spring)
	6. Worn camshaft
	7. Exhaust leak
	8. Ping (detonation)
Clacking noise (like tapping on metal)	**1.** Worn piston pin
	2. Broken piston
	3. Excessive valve clearance
	4. Timing chain hitting cover
Knock (like knocking on a door)	**1.** Rod bearing(s)
	2. Main bearing(s)
	3. Thrust bearing(s)
	4. Loose torque converter
	5. Cracked flex plate (drive plate)
Rattle (like a baby rattle)	**1.** Manifold heat control valve
	2. Broken harmonic balancer
	3. Loose accessory mounts
	4. Loose accessory drive belt or a defective tensioner. See Figure 5–4.
Clatter (like rolling marbles)	**1.** Rod bearings
	2. Piston pin
	3. Loose timing chain
Whine (like an electric motor running)	**1.** Generator (alternator) bearing
	2. Drive belt
	3. Power steering
	4. Belt noise (accessory or timing)
Clunk (like a door closing)	**1.** Engine mount
	2. Drive axle shaft U-joint or constant velocity (CV) joint

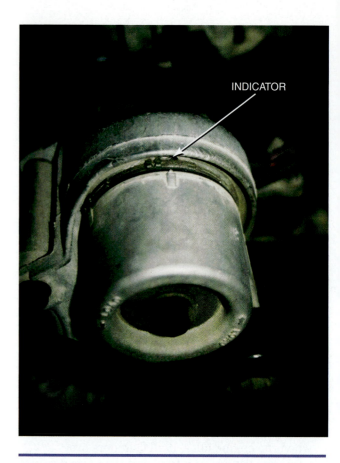

INDICATOR

Figure 5–4 An accessory drive belt tensioner. Most tensioners have a mark that indicates normal operating location. If the belt has stretched, this indicator mark will be outside of the normal range. Anything wrong with the belt or the tensioner can cause noise.

■ VACUUM TEST

Vacuum is pressure below atmospheric pressure and is measured in **inches** (or millimeters) **of Mercury (Hg).** An engine in good mechanical condition will run with high manifold vacuum. Manifold vacuum is developed by the pistons as they move down on the intake stroke to draw the charge from the intake manifold.

Idle Vacuum Test

An engine in proper condition should idle with a steady vacuum between 17 and 21 inches Hg. See Figure 5–5.

> **NOTE:** Engine vacuum readings vary with altitude. A reduction of 1 inch Hg per 1000 feet (300 meters) of altitude should be subtracted from the expected values if testing a vehicle above 1000 feet (300 meters) of altitude.

Figure 5–5 A typical vacuum gauge showing about 19 in. Hg of vacuum at idle—well within the normal reading of 17 to 21 in. Hg.

Low and Steady Vacuum

If the vacuum is lower than normal, yet the gauge reading is steady, the most common causes include

- Retarded ignition timing
- Retarded cam timing (check timing chain for excessive slack or timing belt for proper installation)

Fluctuating Vacuum

If the needle drops then returns to a normal reading, then drops again and then again returns, this indicates a sticking valve. A common cause of sticking valves is lack of lubrication of the valve stems. See Figures 5–6 through 5–16.

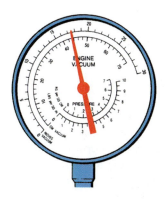

Figure 5–6 An engine in good mechanical condition should produce 17 to 21 in. Hg of vacuum at idle at sea level.

Figure 5–7 A steady but low reading could indicate retarded valve or ignition timing.

Figure 5–8 A gauge reading with the needle fluctuating 3 to 9 in. Hg below normal often indicates a vacuum leak in the intake system.

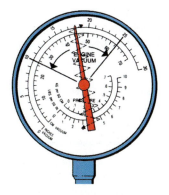

Figure 5–9 A leaking head gasket can cause the needle to vibrate as it moves through a range from below to above normal.

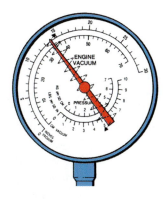

Figure 5–10 An oscillating needle 1 or 2 in. Hg below normal could indicate an incorrect air–fuel mixture (either too rich or too lean).

Figure 5–11 A rapidly vibrating needle at idle that becomes steady as engine speed is increased indicates worn valve guides.

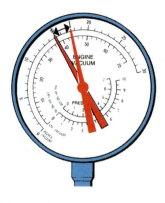

Figure 5–12 If the needle drops 1 or 2 in. Hg from the normal reading, one of the engine valves is burned or not seating properly.

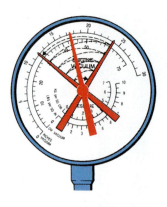

Figure 5–13 Weak valve springs will produce a normal reading at idle, but as engine speed increases, the needle will fluctuate rapidly between 12 and 24 in. Hg.

Figure 5–14 A steady needle reading that drops 2 or 3 in. Hg when the engine speed is increased slightly above idle indicates that the ignition timing is retarded.

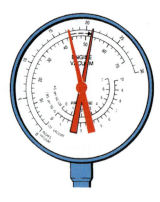

Figure 5–15 A steady needle reading that rises 2 or 3 in. Hg when the engine speed is increased slightly above idle indicates that the ignition timing is advanced.

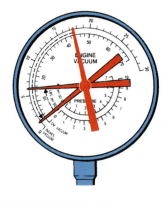

Figure 5–16 A needle that drops to near zero when the engine is accelerated rapidly and then rises slightly to a reading below normal indicates an exhaust restriction.

■ COMPRESSION TEST

Testing an engine for proper compression is one of the fundamental engine diagnostic tests that can be performed. For smooth engine operation, all cylinders must have equal compression. An engine can lose compression by leakage of air through one or more of only three routes:

- Intake or exhaust valve
- Piston rings (or piston, if there is a hole)
- Cylinder head gasket

For best results, the engine should be warmed to normal operating temperature before testing. An accurate compression test should be performed as follows:

1. Remove all spark plugs. This allows the engine to be cranked to an even speed. Be sure to label all spark plug wires.

> **CAUTION:** Disable the ignition system by disconnecting the primary leads from the ignition coil or module or by grounding the coil wire after removing it from the center of the distributor cap. Also disable the fuel-injection system to prevent the squirting of fuel into the cylinder.

2. Block open the throttle and choke (if the vehicle is so equipped). This permits the maximum amount

The Paper Test

A soundly running engine should produce even and steady exhaust at the tail pipe. Hold a piece of paper (even a dollar bill works) or a 3-inch by 5-inch card, within 1 inch (2.5 centimeters) of the tail pipe with the engine running at idle. See Figure 5–17. The paper should blow out evenly without "puffing." If the paper is drawn *toward* the tail pipe at times, the valves in one or more cylinders could be burned. Other reasons why the paper might be sucked toward the tail pipe include the following:

1. The engine could be misfiring because of a lean condition that could occur normally when the engine is cold.
2. Pulsing of the paper toward the tail pipe could also be caused by a hole in the exhaust system.

If exhaust escapes through a hole in the exhaust system, air could be drawn—in the intervals between the exhaust puffs—from the tail pipe to the hole in the exhaust, causing the paper to be drawn toward the tail pipe.

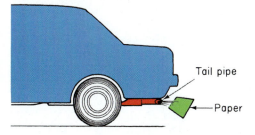

Figure 5–17 The paper test involves holding a piece of paper near the tail pipe of an idling engine. A good engine should produce even outward puffs of exhaust. If the paper is sucked in toward the tail pipe, a burned valve is a possibility.

of air to be drawn into the engine. This step also ensures consistent compression test results.

3. Thread a compression gauge into one spark plug hole and crank the engine. See Figure 5–18. Continue cranking the engine through four compression strokes. Each compression stroke makes a puffing sound.

HINT: Note the reading on the compression gauge after the first puff. This reading should be at least one-half of the final reading. For example, if the final, highest reading is 150 psi, then the reading after the first puff should be higher than 75 psi. A low first-puff reading indicates possible weak, broken, or worn piston rings.

The Hose Trick

Installing spark plugs can be made easier by using a rubber hose on the end of the spark plug. The hose can be a vacuum hose, fuel line, or even an old spark plug wire end. See Figure 5–19. The hose makes it easy to start the threads of the spark plug into the cylinder head. After starting the threads, continue to thread the spark plug for several turns. Using the hose eliminates the chance of cross-threading the plug. This is especially important when installing spark plugs in aluminum cylinder heads.

Figure 5–18 A two-piece compression gauge set. The threaded hose is screwed into the spark plug hole after removing the spark plug. The gauge part is then snapped onto the end of the hose.

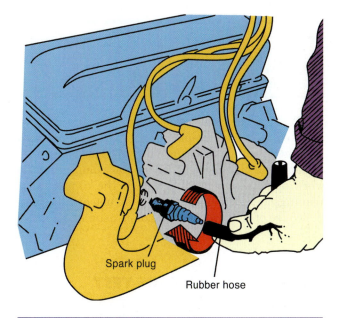

Figure 5–19 Use a vacuum or fuel line hose over the spark plug to install it without danger of cross-threading the cylinder head.

Record the highest readings and compare the results. Most vehicle manufacturers specify the minimum compression reading, the maximum allowable variation among cylinders, and a maximum difference of 20% between the highest reading and the lowest reading. For example,

If the high reading is   150 psi
Subtract 20%   −30 psi
Lowest allowable compression is 120 psi

HINT: To make the math quick and easy, think of 10% of 150, which is 15 (move the decimal point to the left one place). Now double it: $15 \times 2 = 30$. This represents 20%.

NOTE: During cranking, the oil pump cannot maintain normal oil pressure. Extended engine cranking such as occurs during a compression test can cause hydraulic lifters to collapse. When the engine starts, loud valve clicking noises may be heard. This should be considered normal after performing a compression test, and the noise should stop after the vehicle has been driven a short distance.

■ WET COMPRESSION TEST

If the reading of the compression test indicates low compression on one or more cylinders, add two squirts of oil to the cylinder to help seal around the piston rings and retest. This is called a **wet compression test.**

CAUTION: Do not use more oil than three squirts from a hand-operated oil squirt can. Too much oil can cause a hydrostatic lock, which can damage or break pistons or connecting rods or even crack a cylinder head.

Perform the compression test again and observe the results. If the first-puff readings greatly improve and the readings are much higher than they were without the oil, the cause of the low compression is worn or defective piston rings. If the compression readings increase only slightly (or not at all), then the cause of the low compression is usually defective valves. See Figure 5–20.

■ CYLINDER LEAKAGE TEST

One of the best tests that can be used to determine engine condition is the cylinder leakage test. This test involves injecting air under pressure into the cylinders one at a time. The amount and location of

Figure 5–20 Badly burned exhaust valve. A compression test could have detected a problem, and a cylinder leakage test (leak-down test) could have been used to determine the exact problem.

Figure 5–21 A typical hand-held cylinder leakage tester.

any escaping air helps the technician determine the condition of the engine. The air is put into the cylinder through a cylinder leakage gauge inserted in the spark plug hole. See Figure 5–21. To perform the cylinder leakage test, take the following steps:

1. For best results, the engine should be at normal operating temperature (upper radiator hose hot and pressurized).
2. The cylinder being tested must be at top dead center (TDC) of the compression stroke.

NOTE: The greatest amount of wear occurs at the top of the cylinder because of the heat generated near the top. The piston ring flex also adds to the wear at the top of the cylinder.

3. Calibrate the cylinder leakage unit per manufacturer's instructions.
4. Inject air into the cylinders one at a time, rotating the engine by firing order to test each cylinder at TDC on the compression stroke.
5. Evaluate the results:
   - Less than 10% leakage: good
   - Less than 20% leakage: acceptable
   - Less than 30% leakage: poor
   - More than 30% leakage: definite problem

HINT: If leakage seems unacceptably high, repeat the test, making sure that the test is being performed correctly and that the cylinder being tested is at TDC on the compression stroke.

6. Check the source of air leakage.
   - If air is heard escaping from the oil fill cap, the *piston rings* are worn or broken.
   - If air is observed bubbling out of the radiator, there is a possible blown *head gasket* or cracked *cylinder head.*
   - If air is heard coming from the carburetor or air inlet on fuel-injection equipped engines, there is a defective *intake valve(s).*
   - If air is heard coming from the tail pipe, there is a defective *exhaust valve(s).*

CYLINDER POWER BALANCE TEST

Most large engine analyzers have a cylinder power balance feature. The purpose of a cylinder power balance test is to determine if all cylinders are contributing power equally. The equipment measures this by shorting out one cylinder at a time while the engine is running. If the engine speed (RPM) does not drop as much for one cylinder as for other cylinders of the same engine, then the shorted cylinder must be weaker than the other cylinders. For example:

Cylinder Number	RPM Drop When Ignition Is Shorted
1	75
2	70
3	15
4	65
5	75
6	70

Cylinder 3 is the weak cylinder.

NOTE: Most automotive test equipment tests cylinder balance automatically. Be certain to identify the offending cylinder correctly. Cylinder 3 as identified by the equipment may be the third cylinder in the firing order instead of the actual cylinder 3.

POWER BALANCE TEST PROCEDURE

When point-type ignition was used on all vehicles, the common method for determining which, if any, cylinder was weak was to remove a spark plug wire from one spark plug at a time while watching a tachometer and a vacuum gauge. This method is not recommended on any vehicle with any type of electronic ignition. For these vehicles, if any spark plug wires are removed from a spark plug while the engine is running, the ignition coil tries to supply increasing levels of voltage in an attempt to jump the increasing gap as the plug wires are removed. This high voltage could easily damage the ignition coil or the ignition module or both. Many engine analyzers ground the primary of the ignition circuit to perform a cylinder power balance test.

The acceptable method of canceling cylinders, which will work on all types of ignition systems including distributorless, is to *ground* the secondary current for each cylinder by using a test light and short lengths of rubber vacuum hose as shown in Figure 5–22. The cylinder with the least RPM drop is the cylinder not producing its share of power.

Some items that could cause the engine speed to remain steady (no RPM drop) include:

- A defective spark plug wire
- A defective or excessively worn spark plug
- A faulty fuel injector (if individual injectors for each cylinder)
- Burned valve
- Broken valve spring
- Worn cam lobe affecting the opening of the valves
- Bent pushrod (if OHV engine)
- Broken rocker arm (if equipped)
- Hole in the piston or an excessively worn or damaged piston ring

OIL PRESSURE TEST

Proper oil pressure is very important for the operation of any engine. Low oil pressure can cause engine wear, and engine wear can cause low oil pressure.

If the main and rod bearings are worn, oil pressure is reduced because of oil leakage around the

Figure 5–22 Using a vacuum hose and a test light to ground one cylinder at a time on a distributorless ignition system. This works on all types of ignition systems and provides a method for grounding out one cylinder at a time without fear of damaging any component.

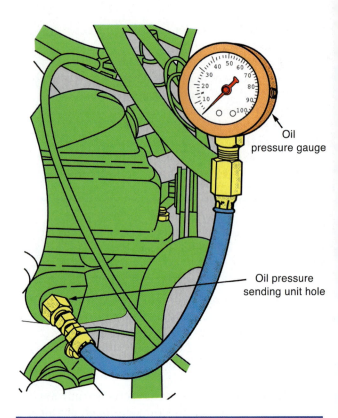

Figure 5–23 To measure engine oil pressure, remove the oil pressure sending (sender) unit usually located near the oil filter. Screw the pressure gauge into the oil pressure sending unit hole.

bearings. Oil pressure testing is usually performed according to the following steps:

1. Operate the engine until normal operating temperature is achieved.
2. With the engine off, remove the oil pressure sending unit or sender, usually located near the oil filter. Thread an oil pressure gauge into the threaded hole. See Figure 5–23.

> **HINT:** An oil pressure gauge can be made from another gauge, such as an old air-conditioning gauge no longer used for air-conditioning work, and a flexible brake hose. The threads are often the same as those used for the oil pressure sending unit.

3. Start the engine and observe the gauge. Record the oil pressure at idle and at 2500 RPM.

Most vehicle manufacturers recommend a minimum oil pressure of 10 psi per 1000 RPM. Therefore, at 2500 RPM, the oil pressure should be at least 25 psi. Always compare your test results with the manufacturers' recommended oil pressure.

In addition to engine bearing wear, other possible causes for low oil pressure include:

- Low oil level
- Diluted oil
- Stuck oil pressure relief valve

■ OIL PRESSURE WARNING LAMP

The red oil pressure warning lamp in the dash usually lights when the oil pressure is less than 4 to 7 psi, depending on vehicle and engine. The oil light should not be on during driving. If the oil warning lamp is on, stop the engine immediately. Always confirm oil pressure with a good and tested mechanical gauge before performing engine repairs because the sending unit or circuit may simply be defective.

■ OIL LEAKS

Oil leaks can lead to severe engine damage if the resulting low oil level is not corrected. Besides causing

What's Leaking?

The color of the leaks observed under a vehicle can help the technician determine and correct the cause. Some leaks such as condensate (water) from the air conditioning system are normal, whereas a brake fluid leak is very dangerous. The following are colors of common leaks:

Sooty black	Engine oil
Yellow, green, blue, or orange	Antifreeze (coolant)
Red	Automatic transmission fluid
Murky brown	Brake or power steering fluid or very neglected antifreeze (coolant)
Clear	Air conditioning condensate (water, normal)

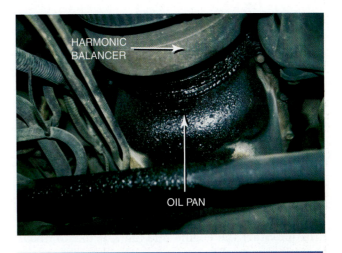

Figure 5–24 What looks like an oil pan gasket leak can be a rocker cover gasket leak. Always look up and look for the highest place you see oil leaking; that should be repaired first.

an oily mess where the vehicle is parked, the oil leak can cause blue smoke to occur under the hood as leaking oil drips on the exhaust system. Finding the location of the oil leak can often be difficult. See Figures 5–24 and 5–25. To help find the source of oil leaks follow these steps:

1. Clean the engine or area around the suspected oil leak. Use a high-powered hot water spray to wash the engine or a coin-operated car wash. Keep the engine running and spray the entire engine and the engine compartment. Avoid letting the water come into direct contact with the air inlet and ignition distributor or ignition coil(s).

HINT: If the engine starts to run rough or stalls when it gets wet, then the secondary ignition wires (spark plug wires) or distributor cap may be defective or have weak insulation. Be certain to wipe all wires and the distributor cap dry with a soft, dry cloth if the engine stalls.

An alternative method is to spray a degreaser on the engine and then start and run the engine until warm. Engine heat helps the degreaser penetrate the grease and dirt. Use a water hose to rinse off the engine and engine compartment.

Figure 5–25 The transmission and flexplate (flywheel) were removed to check the exact location of this oil leak. The rear main seal and/or the oil pan gasket could be the cause of this leak.

CAUTION: Be sure that the floor drains are equipped with the proper oil separator to prevent the waste from getting into the sewer system. Always follow federal, state, provincial, and local regulations.

2. If the oil leak is not visible or oil seems to be coming from "everywhere," sprinkle a white talcum powder on the engine. The leaking oil will show up as a dark area on the white powder. See Tech Tip "The Foot Powder Spray Trick."

Fluorescent dye can also be added to the engine oil. Add about 0.5 oz. (15 cc) of dye per 5 quarts of engine oil. Start the engine and allow it to run about ten minutes to thoroughly mix the dye throughout the engine. A black light then shown around every suspected oil leak area will easily locate any and every leak.

TECH TIP

The Foot Powder Spray Trick

The source of an oil or other fluid leak is often difficult to determine. A quick-and-easy method that works is the following. First, clean the entire area. This can best be done by spraying a commercially available degreaser on the entire area. Let it soak to loosen all accumulated oil and greasy dirt. Clean off the degreaser with a water hose. Let the area dry. Start the engine, and using spray foot powder or other aerosol powder product, spray the entire area. The leak will turn the white powder dark. In this way the exact location of any leak can be quickly determined.

PHOTO SEQUENCE 4 *Performing a Compression Test*

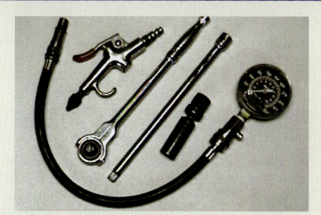

P4–1 The tools and equipment needed to perform a compression test include a compression gauge, an air nozzle, and the socket ratchets and extensions that may be necessary to remove the spark plugs from the engine.

P4–2 To prevent ignition and fuel-injection operation while the engine is being cranked, remove both the fuel-injection fuse and the ignition fuse. If the fuses cannot be removed, disconnect the wiring connectors for the injectors and the ignition system.

P4–3 Block open the throttle (and choke, if the engine is equipped with a carburetor). Here a screwdriver is being used to wedge the throttle linkage open. Keeping the throttle open ensures that enough air will be drawn into the engine so that the compression test results will be accurate.

P4–4 Before removing the spark plugs, use an air nozzle to blow away any dirt that may be around the spark plug. This step helps prevent debris from getting into the engine when the spark plugs are removed.

P4–5 Remove all of the spark plugs. Be sure to mark the spark plug wires so that they can be reinstalled onto the correct spark plugs after the compression test has been performed.

P4–6 Select the proper adapter for the compression gauge. The threads on the adapter should match those on the spark plug.

P4–7 If necessary, connect a battery charger to the battery before starting the compression test. It is important that consistent cranking speed be available for each cylinder being tested.

P4–8 Have an assistant use the ignition key to crank the engine while you are observing the compression gauge. Make a note of the reading on the gauge after the first "puff," which indicates the first compression stroke that occurred on that cylinder as the engine was being rotated. An engine with good piston rings should indicate at least one-half the final reading on the first puff. If the first puff reading is low and the reading gradually increases with each puff, weak or worn piston rings may be indicated.

P4–9 After the engine has been cranked for four "puffs," stop cranking the engine and observe the compression gauge.

P4–10 Record the first puff and this final reading for each cylinder. The final readings should all be within 20% of each other.

P4–11 If a cylinder(s) is lower than most of the others, use an oil can and squirt two squirts of engine oil into the cylinder and repeat the compression test. This is called performing a wet compression test.

P4–12 If the gauge reading is now much higher than the first test results, then the cause of the low compression is due to worn or defective piston rings. The oil in the cylinder temporarily seals the rings, which causes the higher reading.

■ SUMMARY

1. The first step in diagnosing engine condition is to perform a thorough visual inspection, including a check of oil and coolant levels and conditions and checking for abnormal smoke or smells.

2. Many engine-related problems make a characteristic noise.

3. A compression test can be used to test the condition of valves and piston rings.

4. A cylinder leakage test fills the cylinder with compressed air, and the gauge indicates the percentage of leakage.

5. A cylinder balance test indicates whether all cylinders are working equally.

6. Testing engine vacuum is another procedure that can help the service technician determine engine condition.

7. Oil leaks can be found by using a white powder or a fluorescent dye and a black light.

■ REVIEW QUESTIONS

1. List three simple items that could cause engine noises.

2. Describe how to perform a compression test and how to determine what is wrong with an engine based on a compression test result.

3. Describe the cylinder leakage test.

4. Explain how a technician can safely ground out one cylinder at a time without damage to the electronics of the vehicle.

5. Describe how a vacuum gauge would indicate if the valves were sticking in their guides.

■ ASE CERTIFICATION-TYPE QUESTIONS

1. Technician A says that the paper test could detect a burned valve. Technician B says that a hole in the exhaust can cause paper held at the tailpipe to fluctuate. Which technician is correct?
   a. Technician A only
   b. Technician B only
   c. Both Technicians A and B
   d. Neither Technician A nor B

2. Two technicians are discussing oil leaks. Technician A says that an oil leak can be found using a fluorescent dye in the oil with a black light to check for leaks. Technician B says that a white spray powder can be used to locate oil leaks. Which technician is correct?
   a. Technician A only
   b. Technician B only
   c. Both Technicians A and B
   d. Neither Technician A nor B

3. A smoothly operating engine depends on _____.
   a. High compression on most cylinders
   b. Equal compression among cylinders
   c. Cylinder compression levels above 100 psi (700 kPa) and within 70 psi (500 kPa) of each other
   d. Compression levels below 100 psi (700 kPa) on most cylinders

4. A good reading for a cylinder leakage test would be _____.
   a. Within 20% among cylinders
   b. All cylinders below 20% leakage
   c. All cylinders above 20% leakage
   d. All cylinders above 70% leakage and within 7% of each other

5. Technician A says that during a power balance test, the cylinder that causes the biggest RPM drop is the weak cylinder. Technician B says that if one spark plug wire is grounded out and the engine speed does not drop, a weak or dead cylinder is indicated. Which technician is correct?
   a. Technician A only
   b. Technician B only
   c. Both Technicians A and B
   d. Neither Technician A nor B

6. Vacuum at idle speed should be _____.
   a. 2.5 inches Hg or higher
   b. Over 25 inches Hg
   c. 17 to 21 inches Hg
   d. 6 to 16 inches Hg

7. The low oil pressure warning light usually comes on when _____.
   a. An oil change is required
   b. Oil pressure drops dangerously low (4 to 7 psi)
   c. The oil filter bypass valve opens
   d. The oil filter anti-drainback valve opens

8. Technician A says that white smoke can be caused by a defective cylinder head gasket allowing coolant to enter the combustion chamber. Technician B says that white smoke can be caused by the burning of automatic transmission fluid inside the engine. Which technician is correct?
   a. Technician A only
   b. Technician B only
   c. Both Technicians A and B
   d. Neither Technician A nor B

9. Normal oil pressure should be _____.
   a. Above 10 PSI
   b. 10 PSI per 1000 RPM
   c. 30 PSI at idle; 60 PSI at 2000 RPM
   d. 50–100 PSI

10. An engine is misfiring. A power balance test indicates that when the spark to cylinder #4 is grounded, there is no change in the engine speed. Technician A says that a burned valve is a possible cause. Technician B says that a defective cylinder #4 injector or spark plug wire could be the cause. Which technician is correct?
    a. Technician A only
    b. Technician B only
    c. Both Technicians A and B
    d. Neither Technician A nor B

Engine Disassembly, Cleaning, and Crack Detection

The decision to repair an engine should be based on all the information about the engine that is available to the service technician. In some cases, the engine might not be worth repairing. It is the responsibility of the technician to discuss the advantages and disadvantages of the different repair options with the customer.

■ ENGINE REMOVAL

The engine exterior and the engine compartment should be cleaned before work is begun. A clean engine is easier to work on and the cleaning not only helps to keep dirt out of the engine but also minimizes accidental damage from slipping tools. The battery ground cable is disconnected to avoid the chance of electrical shorts. An even better procedure is to remove the battery from the vehicle.

NOTE: Most technicians lightly scribe around the hood hinges prior to removal to make aligning the hood easier during reinstallation.

Working on the top of the engine is made easier if the hood is removed. With fender covers in place, the hood is loosened from the hinges. With a person on each side of the hood to support it, the hood is lifted off as the bolts that hold the hood are removed.

The hood is usually stored on fender covers placed on the top of the vehicle, where it is least likely to be damaged.

The coolant is drained from the radiator and the engine block to minimize the chance of coolant getting into the cylinders when the head is removed. The exhaust manifold is disconnected.

HINT: On some engines, it is easier to remove the exhaust pipe from the manifold. On others, it is easier to separate the exhaust manifold from the head and leave the manifold attached to the exhaust pipe.

On V-type engines, the intake manifold must be removed before the heads can be taken off. In most cases, a number of wires, accessories, hoses, and tubing must be removed before the manifold head can be removed. If the technician is not familiar with the engine, it is a good practice to put tape on each of the items removed, marked with the proper location of each item so that all items can be easily replaced during engine assembly.

A Picture Is Worth a Thousand Words

Take pictures of the engine being serviced with a Polaroid, digital, or video camera. These pictures will be worth their weight in gold when it comes time to reassemble or reinstall the engine. It is very difficult for anyone to remember the *exact* location of every bracket, wire, and hose. Referring back to the photos of the engine before work was started will help you restore the vehicle to like-new condition.

All coolant hoses are removed, and the transmission oil cooler lines are disconnected from the radiator. The radiator mounting bolts are removed, and the radiator is lifted from the engine compartment. This gets the radiator out of the way so that it will not be damaged while you are working on the engine. This is a good time to have the radiator cleaned, while it is out of the chassis.

The air-conditioning compressor can usually be separated from the engine, leaving all air-conditioning hoses securely connected to the compressor and lines. The compressor can be fastened to the side of the engine compartment, where it will not interfere with engine removal. If it is necessary to disconnect the air-conditioning lines, use a refrigerant recovery system to prevent loss of refrigerant to the atmosphere. All open air-conditioning lines should be securely plugged immediately after they are disconnected to keep dirt and moisture out of the system. They should remain plugged until immediately prior to reassembly.

There are two ways to remove the engine:

- The engine can be lifted out of the chassis with the transmission/transaxle attached.
- The transmission/transaxle can be disconnected from the engine and left in the chassis.

Under the vehicle, the drive shaft (propeller shaft) or half shafts are removed and the exhaust pipes disconnected. In some installations, it may be necessary to loosen the steering linkage idler arm to give clearance. The transmission controls, speedome-ter cable wiring, and clutch linkages are disconnected and tagged.

A sling, either a chain or lift cable, is attached to the engine.

> **HINT:** For the best results, use the factory-installed lifting hooks that are attached to the engine. These hooks were used in the assembly plant to install the engine and are usually in the best location to remove the engine.

A hoist is attached to the sling and snugged to take most of the weight. This leaves the engine resting on the mounts. (Most engines use three mounts, one on each side and one at the back of the transmission or at the front of the engine.) The rear crossmember is removed, and on rear-wheel-drive vehicles, the transmission is lowered. The hoist is tightened to lift the engine. The engine will have to nose up as it is removed, and the front of the engine must come almost straight up as the transmission slides from under the floor pan, as illustrated in Figure 6–1. The engine and transmission are hoisted free of the automobile, swung clear, and lowered onto an open floor area.

> **NOTE:** The engine is lowered and removed from underneath on many front-drive vehicles. See Figures 6–2 and 6–3.

■ ENGINE DISASSEMBLY

The following disassembly procedure applies primarily to pushrod engines. The procedure will have to be modified somewhat when working on overhead cam engines. Engines should be cold before disassembly to minimize the chance of warpage.

Remove the manifold hold-down cap screws and nuts, and lift off the manifold.

With the manifold off of the V-type engine, loosen the rocker arms, and remove the pushrods. The usual practice is to leave the lifters in place when doing only a valve job. Remove the head cap screws and lift the head from the block deck.

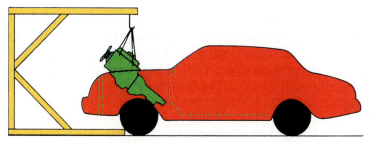

Figure 6–1 An engine must be tipped as it is pulled from the chassis.

Figure 6–2 When removing just the engine from a front-wheel-drive vehicle, the transaxle must be supported. Shown here is a typical fixture that can be used to hold the engine if the transaxle is removed or to hold the transaxle if the engine is removed.

(a)

RACK AND PINION STEERING GEAR

CRADLE

(b)

Figure 6–3 (a) General Motors front-wheel-drive vehicle with the drivetrain (engine and transaxle) removed. (b) The entire cradle, which included the engine, transaxle, and steering gear, was removed and placed onto a stand. The rear cylinder head has been removed to check for the root cause of a coolant leak.

TECH TIP ✔

Use the Proper Disassembly Procedure

When an engine is operated, it builds up internal stresses. Even cast iron parts such as cylinder heads can warp if the proper disassembly procedure is not followed. To disassemble any engine without causing harm, just remember these two important points:

- Disassemble parts from an engine only after it has been allowed to sit for several hours. All engines should be disassembled when the engine is at room temperature.
- Always loosen retaining bolts/nuts in the reverse order of assembly. Most vehicle manufacturers recommend tightening bolts from the center of the component such as a cylinder head toward the outside (ends). Therefore, to disassemble the engine, the outside (outer) bolts should be loosened first, followed by bolts closer to the center.

Taking these steps will help reduce the possibility of warpage occurring when the parts are removed.

cylinders are worn beyond the specified limits, they will have to be rebored to return them to a satisfactory condition.

■ CHECKING CYLINDER BORE

At this point, the cylinder taper and out-of-round of the cylinder bore should be checked just below the ridge and just above the piston when it is at the bottom of the stroke, as shown on the cutaway cylinder in Figure 6–4. These measurements will indicate how much cylinder-wall work is required. If the

■ REMOVING THE OIL PAN

To remove the oil pan, turn the engine upside down. This will be the first opportunity to see the working parts in the bottom end of the engine. Deposits are again a good indication of the condition of the engine and the care it has had. Heavy sludge indicates infrequent oil changes; hard carbon indicates overheating. The oil pump pickup screen should be checked to see how much plugging exists. The con-

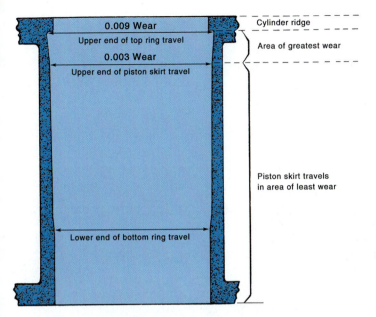

0.009 Wear
Upper end of top ring travel
0.003 Wear
Upper end of piston skirt travel

Cylinder ridge
Area of greatest wear

Piston skirt travels
in area of least wear

Lower end of bottom ring travel

Figure 6–4 Most of the cylinder wear is on the top inch just below the cylinder ridge. This wear is due to the heat and combustion pressures that occur when the piston is near the top of the cylinder. (Courtesy of Dana Corporation, Perfect Circle Products)

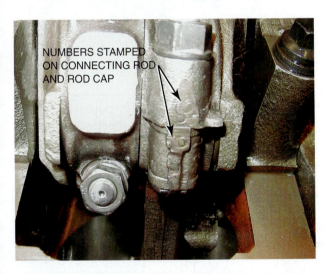

NUMBERS STAMPED ON CONNECTING ROD AND ROD CAP

Figure 6–5 These connecting rods were numbered from the factory.

Figure 6–6 If the rods and mains are not marked, it is wise to use a punch to make identifying marks *before* disassembly of the engine.

necting rods and caps and main bearing caps should be checked to make sure that they are *numbered;* if not, they should be numbered with number stamps or a punch so that they can be reassembled in exactly the same position. See Figures 6–5 and 6–6.

■ REMOVING THE CYLINDER RIDGE

The ridge above the top ring must be removed before the piston and connecting rod assembly is removed. Cylinder wear leaves an upper ridge, and removing it is necessary to avoid catching a ring on the ridge and breaking the piston. Failure to remove the ridge is likely to cause the second piston land to break

when the engine is run after reassembly with new rings, as pictured in Figure 6–7. The ridge is removed with a cutting tool that is fed into the metal ridge. One type of ridge reamer is shown in Figure 6–8. A guide on the tool prevents accidental cutting below the ridge. The reaming job should be done carefully with frequent checks of the work so that no more material than necessary is removed.

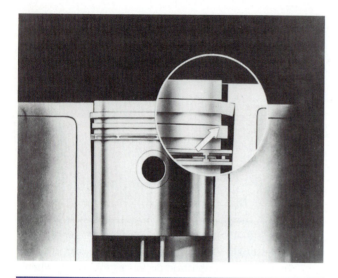

Figure 6–7 If the ridge at the top of a cylinder is not removed, the top piston ring could break the second piston ring land when the piston is pushed out of the cylinder during disassembly, or the second piston ring land could break when the engine is first run after reassembly with new rings. (Courtesy of Sealed Power Corporation)

▪ REMOVING THE PISTONS

Rotate the engine until the piston that is to be removed is at top dead center (TDC). Remove connecting rod nuts from the rod so that the rod cap with its bearing half can be taken out. Fit the rod bolts with protectors to keep the bolt threads from damaging the crankshaft journals, and remove the piston and rod assemblies.

▪ REMOVING THE HARMONIC BALANCER

The next step in disassembly is to remove the coolant pump and the crankshaft **vibration damper** (also called a **harmonic balancer**). First, the bolt and washer that hold the damper are removed. The damper itself should be removed only with a threaded puller similar to the one in Figure 6–9. If a hook-type puller is used around the edge of the damper, it may pull the damper ring from the hub. If this happens, the damper assembly will have to be replaced with a new assembly.

▪ REMOVING THE TIMING CHAIN AND CAMSHAFT

With the damper assembly off, the timing cover can be removed, exposing the timing gear or timing chain. Examine these parts for excessive wear and

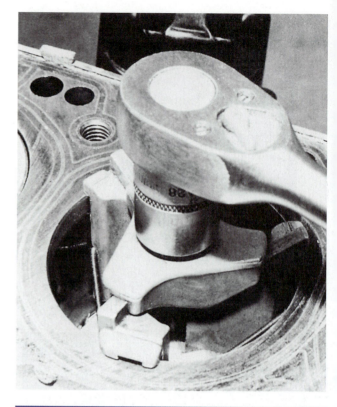

Figure 6–8 Ridge being removed with one type of ridge reamer before the piston assemblies are removed from the engine.

Figure 6–9 Puller being used to pull the vibration damper from the crankshaft.

looseness. A worn timing chain on a high-mileage engine is shown in Figure 6–10. Bolted cam sprockets can be removed to free the timing chain. If camshaft thrust plate retaining screws are used, it will be necessary to remove them.

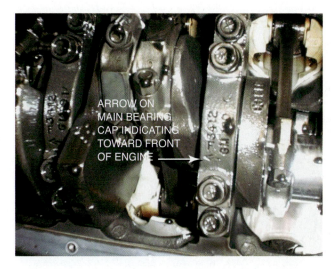

Figure 6–11 Most engines such as this Chevrolet V-8 with 4-bolt main bearing caps have arrows marked on the bearing caps which should point to the front of the engine.

Figure 6–10 Worn timing chain on a high-mileage engine. Notice that the timing chain could "jump a tooth" at the bottom of the smaller crankshaft gear where the chain is in contact with fewer teeth. Notice also that the technician placed all of the bolts back in the block after removal of the part. This procedure helps protect against lost or damaged bolts and nuts.

Figure 6–12 This defective cylinder head gasket was discovered as soon as the head was removed. This cylinder head will require machining or replacement.

The camshaft can be removed at this time, or it can be removed after the crankshaft is out. It must be carefully eased from the engine to avoid damaging the cam bearings or cam lobes. This is done most easily with the front of the engine pointing up. Bearing surfaces are soft and scratch easily, and the cam lobes are hard and chip easily.

the crankshaft is removed, the main bearing caps and bearings are reinstalled on the block to reduce the chance of damage to the caps.

■ REMOVING THE MAIN BEARING AND CRANKSHAFT

The main bearing caps should be checked for position markings before they are removed. They have been machined in place and will not fit perfectly in any other location. See Figure 6–11. After marking, they can be removed to free the crankshaft. When

■ REMOVE AND DISASSEMBLE THE CYLINDER HEAD

Remove the cylinder head retaining bolts by loosening them from the outside toward the center to help prevent the possibility of warpage of the head. Remove the cylinder head(s) and check the head gasket for signs of failure. See Figure 6–12.

Figure 6–13 A valve spring compressor being used to remove the valve keepers (locks).

Figure 6–14 After removing this intake valve, it became obvious why this engine had been running so poorly.

After the heads are removed and placed on the bench, the valves are removed. A C-type valve spring compressor, similar to the one in Figure 6–13, is used to free the **valve locks** or **keepers.** The valve spring compressor is air powered in production shops where valve jobs are done on a regular basis. Mechanical valve spring compressors are used where valve work is done only occasionally. After the valve lock is removed, the compressor is released to free the valve retainer and spring. The spring assemblies are lifted from the head together with any spacers used under them. The parts should be removed in order to aid in diagnosing the exact cause of any malfunction that shows up. The valve tip edge and lock area should be lightly filed to remove any burrs *before* sliding the valve from the head. Burrs will scratch the valve guide.

When all valves have been removed following this procedure for each one, the valve springs, retainers, locks, guides, and seats should be given another visual examination. See Figure 6–14.

■ MECHANICAL CLEANING

Heavy deposits that remain after chemical cleaning will have to be removed by mechanical cleaning. Mechanical cleaning involves scraping, brushing, and abrasive blasting. It should, therefore, be done very carefully on soft metals.

The scraper most frequently used is a **putty knife** or a plastic card. The broad blade of the putty knife helps avoid scratching the surface as it is used to clean the parts. A rotary disc can be used on disassembled parts that will be thoroughly cleaned to

T E C H   T I P

The Wax Trick

Before the engine block can be thoroughly cleaned, all oil gallery plugs must be removed. A popular trick of the trade for plug removal involves heating the plug (not the surrounding metal) with an oxyacetylene torch. The heat tends to expand the plug and make it tighter in the block. Do not overheat.

As the plug is cooling, touch the plug with paraffin wax (beeswax or candle wax may be used). See Figure 6–15. The wax will be drawn down around the threads of the plug by capillary attraction as the plug cools and contracts. After being allowed to cool, the plug is easily removed.

remove the fine abrasive that is part of the plastic bristles. See Figure 6–16.

CAUTION: Do not use a steel wire brush on aluminum parts! Steel is harder than aluminum and will remove some of the aluminum from the surface during cleaning.

■ CHEMICAL CLEANERS

Cleaning chemicals applied to engine parts will mix with and dissolve deposits. The chemicals loosen the deposits so that they can be brushed or rinsed from the surface. A deposit is said to be **soluble** when it can be dissolved with a chemical or solvent.

Most chemical cleaners used for cleaning carbon-type deposits are strong soaps called **caustic materials.** A **pH** value, measured on a scale from 1 to 14, indicates the amount of chemical activity in the soap. The term *pH* is from the French *pouvoir hydrogine,* meaning "hydrogen power." Pure water is neutral; on the pH scale, water is pH 7. Caustic materials have pH numbers from 8 through 14. The higher the number, the stronger the caustic action will be. **Acid materials** have pH numbers from 1 through 6. The lower the number, the stronger the acid action will be. Caustic materials and acid materials neutralize each other. This is what happens when baking soda (a caustic) is used to clean the outside of the battery (an acid surface). The caustic baking soda neutralizes any sulfuric acid that has been spilled or splashed on the outside of the battery.

CAUTION: Whenever working with chemicals, you must use eye protection.

■ SOLVENT-BASED CLEANING

Chemical cleaning can involve a spray washer or a soak in a cold or hot tank. The cleaning solution is usually solvent based, with a medium pH rating of between 10 and 12. Most chemical solutions also contain silicates to protect the metal (aluminum) against corrosion. Strong caustics do an excellent job on cast-iron items but are often too corrosive for aluminum parts. Aluminum cleaners include mineral spirit solvents as well as alkaline detergents.

CAUTION: When cleaning aluminum cylinder heads, blocks, or other engine components, make sure that the chemicals used are "aluminum safe." Many chemicals that are not aluminum safe may turn the aluminum metal black. Try to explain that to a customer!

■ WATER-BASED CHEMICAL CLEANING

Because of environmental concerns, most chemical cleaning is now performed using water-based solutions (called **aqueous-based**). Most aqueous-based chemicals are silicate based and are mixed with water. Aqueous-based solutions can be sprayed on or used in a tank for soaking parts. Aluminum heads and blocks usually require overnight soaking in a solution kept at about 190° F (90° C). For best results, the cleaning solution should be agitated.

PARAFFIN WAX

Figure 6–15 A torch is used to heat gallery plugs. Paraffin wax is then applied and allowed to flow around the threads. This procedure results in easier removal of the plugs and other threaded fasteners that cannot otherwise be loosened.

Figure 6–16 An air-powered grinder attached to a bristle pad being used to clean the gasket surface of a cylinder head. The color of the bristles indicates the grit number. The white is the finest and should be used on aluminum. Yellow is coarse and can be used on aluminum. Green is designed for cast-iron parts only. This type of cleaning pad should not be used on the engine block where the grit could get into the engine oil and cause harm when the engine is started and run after the repair.

■ SPRAY WASHING

A spray washer directs streams of liquid through numerous high-pressure nozzles to dislodge dirt and grime on an engine surface. The force of the liquid hitting the surface, combined with the chemical action of the cleaning solution, produces a clean surface. Spray washing is typically performed in an enclosed washer (like a dishwasher), where parts are rotated on a washer turntable. See Figure 6–17.

Spray washing is faster than soaking. A typical washer cycle is less than thirty minutes per load, compared to eight or more hours for soaking. Most spray washers use an aqueous-based cleaning solution heated to 160° to 180° F (70° to 80° C) with foam suppressants. High-volume remanufacturers use industrial dishwashing machines to clean the disassembled engines' component parts.

■ STEAM CLEANING

Steam cleaners are a special class of sprayers. Steam vapor is mixed with high-pressure water and sprayed on the parts. The heat of the steam and the propellant force of the high-pressure water combine to do the cleaning. Steam cleaning must be used with extreme care. Usually, a caustic cleaner is added to the steam and water to aid in the cleaning. This mixture is so active that it will damage and even remove paint, so painted surfaces must be protected from the spray. Engines are often steam cleaned before they are removed from the chassis.

■ THERMAL CLEANING

Thermal cleaning uses heat to vaporize and char dirt into a dry, powdery ash. Thermal cleaning is best suited for cleaning cast iron, where temperatures as high as 800° F (425° C) are used, whereas aluminum should not be heated to over 600° F (315° C).

The major advantages of thermal cleaning include the following:

1. This process cleans the inside as well as the outside of the casting or part.
2. The waste generated is nonhazardous and is easy to dispose of. However, the heat in the oven usually discolors the metal, leaving it looking dull.

A **pyrolytic** (high-temperature) oven cleans engine parts by decomposing dirt, grease, and gaskets with heat in a manner similar to that of a self-cleaning oven. This method of engine part cleaning

Figure 6–17 A pressure jet washer is similar to a large industrial-sized dishwasher. The part(s) is then rinsed with water to remove chemicals or debris that may remain on the part while it is still in the tank.

is becoming the most popular because there is no hazardous waste associated with it. Labor costs are also reduced because the operator does not need to be present during the actual cleaning operation. See Figure 6–18.

■ COLD TANK CLEANING

The cold soak tank is used to remove grease and carbon. The disassembled parts are placed in the tank so that they are *completely* covered with the chemical cleaning solution. After a soaking period, the parts are removed and rinsed until the milky appearance of the emulsion is gone. The parts are then dried with compressed air. The clean, dry parts are then usually given a very light coating of clean oil to prevent rusting. Carburetor cleaner, purchased with a basket in a bucket, is one of the most common types of cold soak agents in the automotive shop. Usually, there will be a layer of water over the chemical to prevent evaporation of the chemical. This water layer is called a **hydroseal.**

Parts washers are often used in place of soaking tanks. This equipment can move parts back and forth through the cleaning solution or pumps the cleaning solution over the parts. This movement, called **agitation,** keeps fresh cleaning solution moving past the soil to help it loosen. The parts washer is usually equipped with a safety cover held open by a low-temperature **fusible link.** If a fire occurs, the fusible link will melt and the cover will drop closed to snuff the fire out.

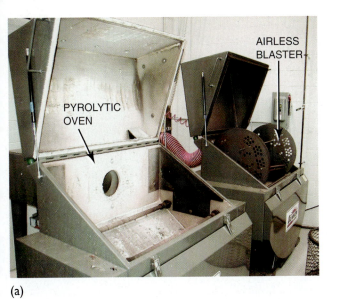

PYROLYTIC OVEN

AIRLESS BLASTER

(a)

(b)

Figure 6–18 (a) A pyrolytic (high temperature) oven cleans by baking the engine parts. After the parts have been cleaned, they are then placed into an airless blaster. This unit uses a paddle to scoop stainless steel shot from a reservoir and forces it against the engine part. The parts must be free of grease and oil to function correctly. (b) Stainless steel shot used in an airless blaster.

■ HOT TANK CLEANING

The hot soak tank is used for cleaning heavy organic deposits and rust from iron and steel parts. The caustic cleaning solution used in the hot soak tank is heated to near 200° F (93° C) for rapid cleaning action. The solution must be inhibited when aluminum is to be cleaned. After the deposits have been loosened, the parts are removed from the tank and rinsed with hot water or steam cleaned, which dries them rapidly. They must then be given a light coating of oil to prevent rusting.

> **HINT: Fogging oil** from a spray can does an excellent job of coating metal parts to keep them from rusting.

■ VAPOR CLEANING

Vapor cleaning is popular in some automotive service shops. The parts to be cleaned are suspended in hot vapors above a perchloroethylene solution. The vapors of the solution loosen the soil from the metal so that it can be blown, wiped, or rinsed from the surface.

■ ULTRASONIC CLEANING

Ultrasonic cleaning is used to clean small parts that must be absolutely clean; for example, hydraulic

lifters and diesel injectors. The disassembled parts are placed in a tank of cleaning solution which is then vibrated at ultrasonic speeds to loosen all the soil from the parts. The soil goes into the solution or falls to the bottom of the tank.

■ VIBRATORY CLEANING

The vibratory method of cleaning is best suited for small parts. Parts are loaded into a vibrating bin with small odd-shaped ceramic or steel pieces, called media, with a cleaning solution of mineral spirits or water-based detergents that usually contain a lubricant additive to help the media pieces slide around more freely. The movement of the vibrating solution and the scrubbing action of the media do an excellent job of cleaning metal.

■ BLASTERS

Cleaning cast-iron or aluminum engine parts with solvents or heat usually requires another operation to achieve a uniform surface finish. Blasting the parts with steel, cast-iron, aluminum, or stainless-steel shot or glass beads is a simple way to achieve a matte or satin surface finish on the engine parts. To keep the shot or beads from sticking to the parts, they must be dry, without a trace of oil or grease, prior to blasting. This means that blasting is the second cleaning method, after the part has been precleaned in a tank, spray washer, or oven. Some blasting is done automatically in an airless shot-blasting machine. Another method is to hard-blast parts in a sealed cabinet. See Figure 6–19.

CAUTION: Glass beads often remain in internal passages of engine parts, where they can come loose and travel through the cylinders when the engine is started. Among other places, these small, but destructive, beads can easily be trapped under the oil baffles of rocker covers and in oil pans and piston-ring grooves. To help prevent the glass beads from sticking, make sure that the parts being cleaned are free of grease and dirt and completely dry.

■ VISUAL INSPECTION

After the parts have been thoroughly cleaned, they should be re-examined for defects. A magnifying glass is helpful in finding defects. Critical parts of a performance engine should be checked for cracks using specialized magnetic or penetration inspection equipment. Internal parts such as pistons, connecting rods, and crankshafts that have cracks should be replaced. Cracks in the block and heads, however, can often be repaired, and these repair procedures are described in a later section.

■ MAGNETIC CRACK INSPECTION

Checking for cracks using a magnetic field is commonly called Magnafluxing, a brand name. Cracks in engine blocks, cylinder heads, crankshafts, and other engine components are sometimes difficult to find during a normal visual inspection, which is why all remanufacturers and most engine builders use a crack detection procedure on all critical engine parts.

Magnetic flux testing is the method most often used on steel and iron components. A metal engine part (such as a cast-iron cylinder head) is connected to a large electromagnet. Magnetic lines of force are easily conducted through the iron part and concentrate on the edges of a crack. A fine iron powder is then applied to the part being tested, and the powder will be attracted to the strong magnetic concentration around the crack. See Figures 6–20 through 6–22.

■ DYE-PENETRANT TESTING

Dye-penetrant testing is usually used on pistons and other parts constructed of aluminum or other non-

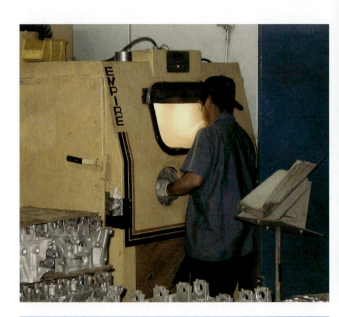

Figure 6–19 Small engine parts can be blasted clean in a sealed cabinet.

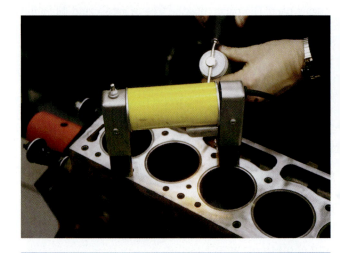

Figure 6–20 The top deck surface of a block being tested using magnetic crack inspection equipment.

magnetic material. A dark-red penetrating chemical is first sprayed on the component being tested. After cleaning, a white powder is sprayed over the test area. If a crack is present, the red dye will stain the white powder. Even though this method will also work on iron and steel (magnetic) parts, it is usually used only on nonmagnetic parts because magnetic methods do not work on these parts.

■ FLUORESCENT-PENETRANT TESTING

To be seen, fluorescent penetrant requires a black light. It can be used on iron, steel, or aluminum

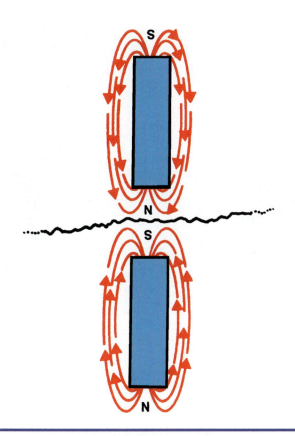

Figure 6–21 If the lines of force are interrupted by a break (crack) in the casting, two magnetic fields are created and the powder will lodge in the crack.

parts. Cracks show up as bright lines when viewed with a black light. The method is commonly called **Zyglo,** a trademark of the Magnaflux Corporation.

■ PRESSURE TESTING

Cylinder heads and blocks are often pressure tested with air and checked for leaks. All coolant passages are blocked with rubber plugs or gaskets, and compressed air is applied to the water jacket(s). The head or block is then lowered into water, where air bubbles indicate a leak. For more accurate results, the water should be heated because the hot water expands the casting by about the same amount as an operating engine would. An alternative method involves running heated water with a dye through the cylinder or block. Any leaks revealed by the dyed water indicate a crack. See Figures 6–23 and 6–24.

■ CRACK REPAIR

Cracks in the engine block can cause coolant to flow into the oil or oil into the coolant. A cracked block can

Figure 6–22 This crack in a vintage Ford 289, V-8 block was likely caused by the technician using excessive force trying to remove the plug from the block. The technician should have used heat and wax, not only to make the job easier, but also to prevent damaging the block.

also cause coolant to leak externally from a crack that goes through to a coolant passage. Cracks in the head will allow coolant to leak into the engine, or they will allow combustion gases to leak into the coolant. Cracks across the valve seat cause hot spots on the valve, which will burn the valve face. A head with a crack will either have to be replaced or the crack will have to be repaired. Two common methods of crack repair are welding and plugging.

> **NOTE:** A hole can be drilled at each end of the crack to keep it from extending further, a step sometimes called **stop drilling.** Cracks that do not cross oil passages, bolt holes, or seal surfaces can sometimes be left alone if stopped.

■ CRACK-WELDING CAST IRON

It takes a great deal of skill to weld cast iron. The cast iron does not puddle or flow as steel does when it is heated. Heavy cast parts, such as the head and block, conduct heat away from the weld so fast that it is difficult to get the part hot enough to melt the iron for welding. When it does melt, a crack will often develop next to the edge of the weld bead. Welding can be done satisfactorily when the entire cast part is heated red hot.

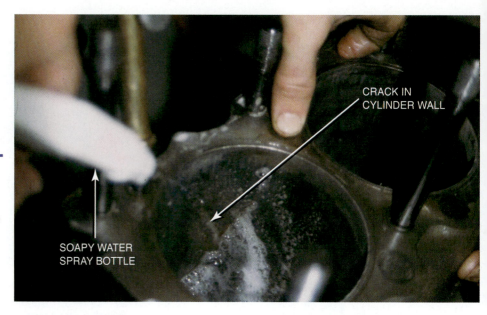

Figure 6–23 To make sure that the mark observed in the cylinder wall was a crack, compressed air was forced into the water jacket while soapy water was sprayed on the cylinder wall. Bubbles confirmed that the mark was indeed a crack.

Figure 6–24 A cylinder head is under water and being pressure tested using compressed air. Note that the air bubbles indicate a crack.

A new technique involves flame welding using a special torch. See Figure 6–25.

CRACK-WELDING ALUMINUM

Cracks in aluminum can be welded using a Heli-arc® or similar welder that is specially designed to weld aluminum. The crack should be cut or burned out before welding begins. The old valve-seat insert should be removed if the crack is in or near the combustion chamber.

CRACK PLUGGING

In the process of crack plugging, a crack is closed using interlocking tapered plugs. This procedure can be performed to repair cracks in both aluminum and cast-iron engine components. The ends of the crack are center punched and drilled with the proper size of tap drill for the plugs. The hole is reamed with a tapered reamer (Figure 6–26) and is then tapped to give full threads (Figure 6–27). The plug is coated with sealer; then it is tightened into the hole (Figure 6–28), sawed about one-fourth of the way through, and broken off. The saw slot controls the breaking point (Figure 6–29). If the plug should break below the surface, it will have to be drilled out and a new plug installed. The plug should go to the full depth or thickness of the cast metal. After the first plug is installed on each end, a new hole is drilled with the tap drill so that it cuts into the edge of the first plug. This new hole is reamed and tapped, and a plug is inserted as before. The plug should fit about one-fourth of the way into the first plug to lock it into

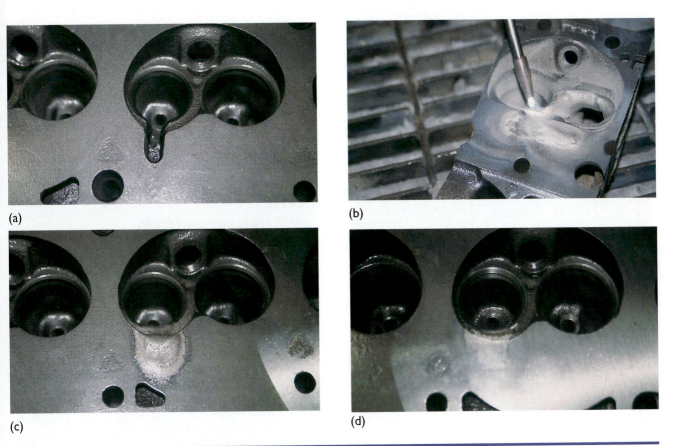

(a) (b)

(c) (d)

Figure 6–25 (a) Before welding, the crack is ground out using a carbide grinder.
(b) Here the technician is practicing using the special cast-iron welding torch before
welding the cracked cylinder head. (c) The finished welded crack before final machining.
(d) The finished cylinder head after the crack has been repaired using welding.

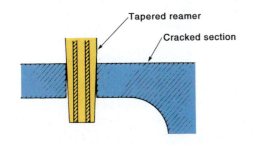

Figure 6–26 Reaming a hole for a tapered plug.

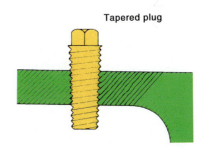

Figure 6–28 Screwing a tapered plug in the hole.

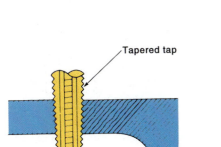

Figure 6–27 Tapping a tapered hole for a plug.

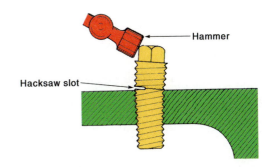

Figure 6–29 Cutting the plug with a hacksaw.

place (Figure 6–30). Interlocking plugs are placed along the entire crack, alternating slightly from side to side. The exposed ends of the plugs are peened over with a hammer to help secure them in place. The surface of the plugs is then ground or filed down nearly to the gasket surface. In the combustion chamber and at the ports, the plugs are ground down to the original surface using a hand grinder. The gasket surface of the head must be resurfaced after the crack has been repaired. See Figure 6–31 for an example of a cylinder head repair using plugs.

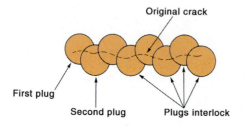

Figure 6–30 Interlocking plugs.

(a)

(b)

(c)

Figure 6–31 (a) A hole is drilled and tapped for the plugs. (b) The plugs are installed. (c) After final machining, the cylinder head can be returned to useful service.

PHOTO SEQUENCE 5   Checking a Cylinder Head for Cracks

P5–1 A strong electromagnet can be used to check a cast-iron cylinder head for cracks. The cylinder head should be thoroughly cleaned and placed on a work surface that gives good visibility.

P5–2 Turn the electromagnet on using the switch at the top and spray a fine iron powder between the poles of the magnet. The magnetic lines of force are more concentrated on the edges of a crack, and the iron powder will be attracted to the strong magnetic concentration around the crack.

P5–3 Pay particular attention to the area around and between the valve seats.

P5–4 This cylinder head has cracks running from two valve seats. The head will either have to be replaced or repaired.

◼ SUMMARY

1. The factory-installed lifting hooks should be used when hoisting an engine.

2. Engine component parts should only be removed when the engine is cold. Also, the torque table should always be followed backward, starting with the highest-number head bolt and working toward the lowest-number. This procedure helps prevent warpage.

3. The ridge at the top of the cylinder should be removed before removing the piston(s) from the cylinder.

4. The connecting rod and main bearing caps should be marked before removing to ensure that they can be re-installed in the exact same location when the engine is reassembled.

5. The tip of the valve stem should be filed before removing valves from the cylinder head to help prevent damage to the valve guide.

6. Mechanical cleaning with scrapers or wire brushes is used to remove deposits.

7. Steel wire brushes should never be used to clean aluminum parts.

8. Most chemical cleaners are strong soaps called caustic materials.

9. Always use aluminum-safe chemicals when cleaning aluminum parts or components.

10. Thermal cleaning is done in a pyrolytic oven in temperatures as high as 800° F (425° C) to turn grease and dirt into harmless ash deposits.

11. Blasters use metal shot or glass beads to clean parts. All of the metal shot or glass beads must be cleaned from the part so as not to cause engine problems.

12. All parts should be checked for cracks using magnetic, dye-penetrant, fluorescent-penetrant, or pressure testing methods.

13. Cracks can be repaired by welding or by plugging.

◼ REVIEW QUESTIONS

1. When should the factory-installed lifting hooks be used?

2. Explain why the cylinder bore should be measured for taper and out-of-round before continuing with an engine disassembly.

3. State two reasons for the removal of the ridge at the top of the cylinder.

4. Explain why the burrs must be removed from valves before removing the valves from the cylinder head.

5. Describe five methods that could be used to clean engines or engine parts.

6. Explain magnetic crack inspection, dye-penetrant testing, and fluorescent-penetrant testing methods and where each can be used.

◼ ASE CERTIFICATION-TYPE QUESTIONS

1. Technician A says that the intake and exhaust manifolds have to be removed before removing the engine from the vehicle. Technician B says that it is often easier to remove the engine from underneath rather than remove the engine from the top of the vehicle. Which technician is correct?
   a. Technician A only
   b. Technician B only
   c. Both Technicians A and B
   d. Neither Technician A nor B

2. Lifting hooks are often installed at the factory because _____.
   a. They make removing the engine easier for the technician.
   b. They are used to install the engine at the factory.
   c. They are part of the engine and should not be removed.
   d. They make servicing the top of the engine easier for the technician.

3. The ridge at the top of the cylinder _____.
   a. Is caused by wear at the top of the cylinder by the rings
   b. Represents a failure of the top piston ring to correctly seal against the cylinder wall
   c. Should not be removed before removing pistons except when reboring the cylinders
   d. Means that a crankshaft with an incorrect stroke was installed in the engine

4. Before the timing chain can be inspected and removed, the following component(s) must be removed:
   a. Rocker cover (valve cover)
   b. Vibration damper
   c. Cylinder head(s)
   d. Intake manifold (V-type engines only)

5. Before the valves are removed from the cylinder head, what operations need to be completed?
   a. Remove valve locks (keepers)
   b. Remove cylinder head(s) from the engine
   c. Remove burrs from the stem of the valve(s)
   d. All of the above

6. Cleaning chemicals are usually either a caustic material or an acid material. Which of the following statements is true?
   a. Both caustics and acids have a pH of 7 if rated according to distilled water.
   b. An acid is lower than 7 and a caustic is higher than 7 on the pH scale.
   c. An acid is higher than 7 and a caustic is lower than 7 on the pH scale.
   d. Pure water is a 1 and a strong acid is a 14 on the pH scale.

7. Many cleaning methods involve chemicals that are hazardous to use and expensive to dispose of after use. The least hazardous method is generally considered to be the _____.
    a. Pyrolytic oven
    b. Hot vapor tank
    c. Hot soak tank
    d. Cold soak tank

8. Magnetic crack inspection _____.
    a. Uses a red dye to detect cracks in aluminum
    b. Uses a black light to detect cracks in iron parts
    c. Uses a fine iron powder to detect cracks in iron parts
    d. Uses a magnet to remove cracks from iron parts

9. Technician A says that engine parts should be cleaned before a thorough test can be done to detect cracks. Technician B says that pressure testing can be used to find cracks in blocks or cylinder heads. Which technician is correct?
    a. Technician A only
    b. Technician B only
    c. Both Technicians A and B
    d. Neither Technician A nor B

10. Plugging can be used to repair cracks_____.
    a. In cast-iron cylinder heads
    b. In aluminum cylinder heads
    c. In both cast-iron and aluminum cylinder heads
    d. Only in cast-iron blocks

Cooling and Lubrication Systems

Satisfactory cooling system operation depends on the design and operating conditions of the system. Unfortunately, the cooling system is usually neglected until there is a problem. Proper routine maintenance can prevent problems.

■ PURPOSE AND FUNCTION OF THE COOLING SYSTEM

The cooling system must allow the engine to warm up to the required operating temperature as rapidly as possible and then maintain that temperature. It must be able to do this when the outside air temperature is as low as −30° F (−35° C) and as high as 110° F (45° C).

Peak combustion temperatures in the engine cycle run from 4000° F to 6000° F (2200° C to 3300° C). The combustion temperatures will *average* between 1200° F and 1700° F (650° and 925° C). Continued temperatures as high as these would weaken engine parts, so heat must be removed from the engine. The cooling system keeps the head and cylinder walls at a temperature that is within the range for maximum efficiency. See Figure 7–1.

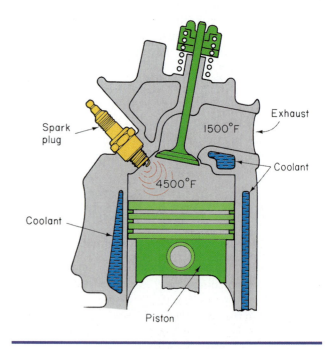

Figure 7–1 Typical combustion and exhaust temperatures.

Overheating Can Be Expensive

A faulty cooling system seems to be a major cause of engine failure. Engine rebuilders often have nightmares about seeing their rebuilt engine placed back in service in a vehicle with a clogged radiator. Most engine technicians routinely replace the water pump and all hoses after an engine overhaul or repair. The radiator should also be checked for leaks and proper flow whenever the engine is repaired or replaced. Overheating is one of the most common causes of engine failure.

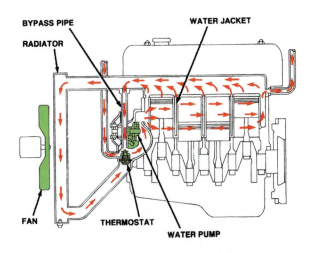

Figure 7–2 A typical cooling system showing how the coolant flows through the block first, then through the cylinder head, and finally through the radiator after the thermostat opens. Notice that coolant flows through the heater core even when the thermostat is closed.

■ COOLING SYSTEM DESIGN

Coolant flows through the engine, where it picks up heat. It then flows to the radiator, where the heat is given up to the outside air. The coolant continually recirculates through the cooling system, as illustrated in Figures 7–2 and 7–3. Its temperature rises as much as 15° F (8° C) as it goes through the engine; then it cools back down as it goes through the radiator. *The coolant flow rate may be as high as one gallon (four liters) per minute for each horsepower the engine produces.*

Hot coolant comes out of the thermostat housing on the top of the engine. The engine coolant outlet is connected to the top of the radiator by the upper hose and clamps. The coolant in the radiator is cooled by air flowing through the radiator. Cool coolant leaves the radiator through an outlet and lower hose, going

Engine Temperature and Exhaust Emissions

Many areas of the United States and Canada have exhaust emission testing. Hydrocarbon (HC) emissions are simply unburned gasoline. To help reduce HC emissions and to pass emission tests, be sure that the engine is at normal operating temperature. Vehicle manufacturers' definition of "normal operating temperature" includes the following:

- Upper radiator hose is hot and pressurized
- Electric cooling fan(s) cycles twice

For best results, the vehicle should be driven about 20 *miles* (32 kilometers) to be certain that the catalytic converter and engine oil, as well as the coolant, are at normal temperature.

Figure 7–3 A Northstar V-8 with the cylinder head removed shows the coolant passages around the cylinder.

into the inlet side of the water pump, where it is recirculated through the engine. The flow of cool air through the radiator is aided by a belt- or electric motor-driven cooling fan.

■ THERMOSTAT TEMPERATURE CONTROL

There is a normal operating temperature range between low-temperature and high-temperature extremes. The thermostat controls the minimum normal temperature. The thermostat is a temperature-controlled valve placed at the engine coolant outlet. See Figure 7–4.

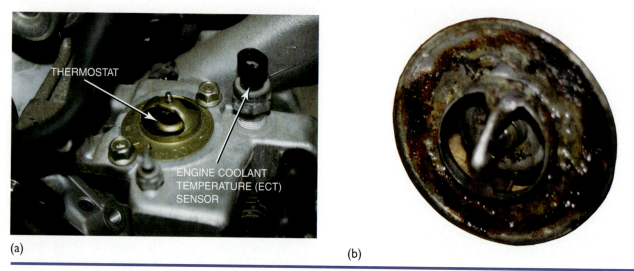

(a)

(b)

Figure 7–4 (a) Typical thermostat located in the intake manifold with the thermostat housing removed. (b) A thermostat that is stuck in the open position. This caused the engine to operate too cold and the vehicle failed an exhaust emission test because of this defect.

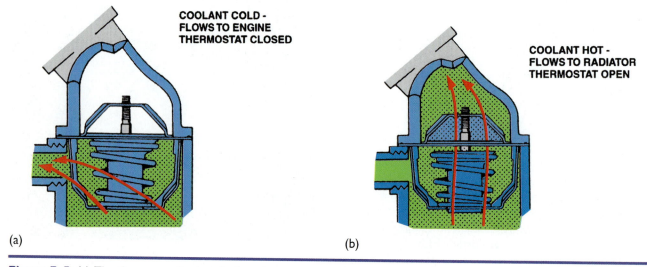

COOLANT COLD - FLOWS TO ENGINE THERMOSTAT CLOSED

COOLANT HOT - FLOWS TO RADIATOR THERMOSTAT OPEN

(a)

(b)

Figure 7–5 (a) The thermostat is closed when the engine is cold, and the coolant flows through the bypass passage thereby bypassing the thermostat. (b) When the thermostat opens, most of the coolant flows through the thermostat to the radiator.

NOTE: Some engine designs place the thermostat at the inlet side of the water pump.

An encapsulated, wax-based, plastic-pellet heat sensor is located on the engine side of the thermostatic valve. As the engine warms, heat swells the heat sensor and a mechanical link connected to the heat sensor opens the thermostat valve. As the thermostat begins to open, it allows some coolant to flow to the radiator, where it is cooled. The remaining part of the coolant continues to flow through the **by-** **pass,** thereby bypassing the thermostat and flowing back through the engine. See Figure 7–5. The rated temperature of the thermostat indicates the temperature at which the thermostat starts to open. The thermostat is fully open at about 20° higher than its opening temperature. See the following examples.

Thermostat Opening Temperature	Starts to Open	Fully Open
180° F (82° C)	180° F (82° C)	200° F (93° C)
195° F (91° C)	195° F (91° C)	215 °F (102° C)

Figure 7–6 Is this engine operating at the correct temperature? This is a Canadian Pontiac Grand Prix. This gauge shows about 91° C or 195° F, which is about the opening temperature of the thermostat.

If the radiator, water pump, and coolant passages are functioning correctly, the engine should always be operating within the opening and fully open temperature range of the thermostat. See Figure 7–6.

An infrared pyrometer can be used to measure the temperature of the coolant near the thermostat. The area on the engine side of the thermostat should be at the highest temperature that exists in the engine.

HINT: For a more accurate reading while using an infrared temperature probe, place some black electrical tape on the area to be tested. Because the infrared depends on a reflective surface to determine the temperature, the black surface makes the readings more accurate.

A properly operating cooling system should cause the pyrometer to read as follows:

1. As the engine warms up, the temperature reaches near thermostat-opening temperature.
2. As the thermostat opens, the temperature drops just as the thermostat opens, sending coolant to the radiator.
3. As the thermostat cycles, the temperature should range between the opening temperature of the thermostat and 20° F (11° C) above the opening temperature. See Figures 7–7 and 7–8.

Figure 7–7 A cutaway of a small block Chevrolet V-8 showing the passage from the cylinder head through the front of the intake manifold to the thermostat.

NOTE: If the temperature rises higher than 20°F (11° C) above the opening temperature of the thermostat, inspect the cooling system for a restriction or low coolant flow. A clogged radiator could also cause the excessive temperature rise.

Figure 7–8 Some thermostats are an integral part of the housing and are replaced as an assembly.

A scan tool can be used on many vehicles to read the actual temperature of the coolant as detected by the engine coolant temperature (ECT) sensor. Although the sensor or the wiring to and from the sensor may be defective, at least the scan tool can indicate what the computer "thinks" the coolant temperature is.

> **HINT:** An overheating engine *may* result from a faulty thermostat. An engine that does not get warm enough *always* indicates a faulty thermostat.

■ COOLANT

Organic acid technology (OAT) antifreeze coolant does not contain silicates or phosphates. This type of coolant is usually orange in color and was first developed by Havoline (called **DEX-COOL**) and used in General Motors vehicles starting in 1996.

Hybrid organic acid technology (HOAT) is a newer variation of this technology and is similar to the OAT-type antifreeze as it uses additives that are not abrasive to water pumps, yet provide the correct pH. The pH of the coolant is usually above 11. A pH of 7 is neutral with lower numbers indicating an acidic solution and higher numbers indicating a caustic solution. If the pH is too high, the coolant can cause scaling and reduce the heat transfer ability of the coolant. If the pH is too low, the resulting acidic solution could cause corrosion of the engine components exposed to the coolant.

T E C H   T I P

Ignore the Windchill Factor

Windchill is a factor that combines the actual temperature and the wind speed to determine the overall heat loss effect on bare skin. Because it is the heat loss factor for bare skin, the windchill temperature is *not* to be considered when determining antifreeze protection levels.

Although moving air does make it feel colder, the actual temperature is not changed by the wind and the engine coolant will not be affected by the windchill. Not convinced? Try this. Place a thermometer in a room and wait until a stable reading is obtained. Then turn on a fan and have the air blow across the thermometer. The temperature will not change.

Testing the Coolant with a Hydrometer

Coolant can be checked using a coolant hydrometer, which measures the density of the coolant. The higher the density, the more concentration of antifreeze in the water. Most coolant hydrometers read the freezing point and boiling point of the coolant. See Figure 7–9. For best results, the coolant should have a freezing point lower than $-34°$ F ($-37°$ C) and a boiling point above $234°$ F ($112°$ C).

Coolant Replacement

Many vehicle manufacturers recommend coolant replacement every two to three years or every 24,000 to 36,000 miles depending on make and model. The trend to use long-life coolant has extended the change interval to 100,000 miles or longer.

Recycling and Disposing of Used Coolant

Coolant (antifreeze and water) should be recycled. Used coolant may contain heavy metals, such as lead, aluminum, and iron, that are absorbed by the coolant during its use in the engine.

Recycle machines filter out these metals and dirt and reinstall the depleted additives. The recycled coolant, restored to be like new, can be reinstalled into the vehicle.

> **CAUTION:** Most vehicle manufacturers warn that antifreeze coolant should not be reused unless it is recycled and the additives restored.

Figure 7–9 Checking the freezing and boiling protection levels of the coolant using a hydrometer.

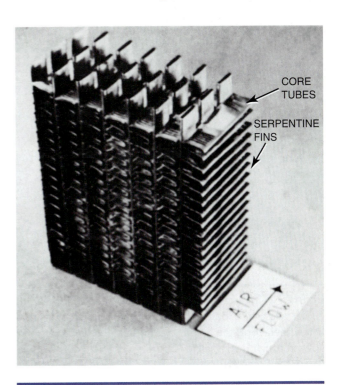

CORE TUBES

SERPENTINE FINS

AIR FLOW

Figure 7–10 Section from a serpentine core radiator. (Courtesy of Modine Manufacturing Company)

Used coolant drained from vehicles should be disposed of according to federal, state, and local laws. Check with recycling companies authorized by local or state government for the exact method recommended for disposal in your area.

■ THE DESIGN AND FUNCTION OF THE RADIATOR

Two types of radiator cores are in common use in domestic vehicles—the serpentine fin core and the plate fin core. In each of these types the coolant flows through oval-shaped **core tubes.** Heat is transferred through the tube wall and soldered joint to **fins.** The fins are exposed to airflow, which removes heat from the radiator and carries it away. See Figures 7–10 and 7–11.

Most automobile radiators are made from yellow brass or aluminum. These materials are corrosion resistant, have good heat-transferring ability, and are easily formed.

Core tubes are made from 0.0045- to 0.012-inch (0.1- to 0.3-millimeter) sheet brass or aluminum. The metal is rolled into round tubes and the joints are sealed with a locking seam.

The radiator must be capable of removing an amount of heat energy approximately equal to the heat energy of the power produced by the engine.

Figure 7–11 Cutaway of a typical radiator showing restriction of tubes. Changing antifreeze frequently helps prevent this type of problem.

Each horsepower is equivalent to 42 BTU (10,800 calories) per minute.

Radiator headers and tanks that close off the ends of the core are made of sheet brass 0.020 to 0.050 inches (0.5 to 1.25 millimeters) thick or of molded plastic. When a transmission oil cooler is used in the radiator, it is placed in the outlet tank, where the coolant has the lowest temperature (Figure 7–12).

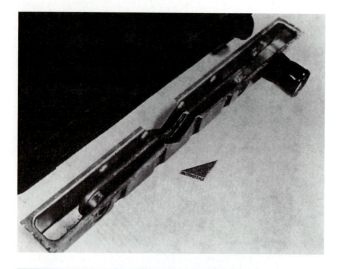

Figure 7–12 Cutaway showing an automatic transmission cooler passage inside the radiator. Air cools the coolant, which then cools the automatic transmission fluid that flows through the radiator. (Courtesy of The Dow Chemical Company)

The Cooling System Pressure Cap

The filler neck or reservoir of the radiator is fitted with a pressure cap. The cap has a spring-loaded valve that closes the cooling system vent, which causes cooling pressure to build up to the pressure setting of the cap. At this point, the valve will release the excess pressure to prevent system damage. See Figure 7–13.

Engine cooling systems are pressurized to raise the boiling temperature of the coolant. *The boiling temperature will increase by approximately 3°F (1.6°C) for each pound of increase in pressure.* At standard atmospheric pressure, water will boil at 212°F (100°C). With a 15 psi (100 kPa) pressure cap, water will boil at 257°F (125°C), which is a maximum operating temperature for an engine. With the proper antifreeze/water mixture, the boiling point should exceed 270°F (132°C) when under 15 psi of pressure.

> **NOTE:** The proper operation of the pressure cap is especially important at high altitudes. The boiling point of water is lowered by about 1° F for every 550-foot increase in altitude. Therefore, in Denver, Colorado (altitude 5280 feet), the boiling point of water is about 202° F, and at the top of Pike's Peak in Colorado (14,110 feet) water boils at 186° F.

■ COOLANT RECOVERY SYSTEM

Excess pressure usually forces some coolant from the system through an overflow. Most cooling systems connect the overflow to a plastic reservoir to hold ex-

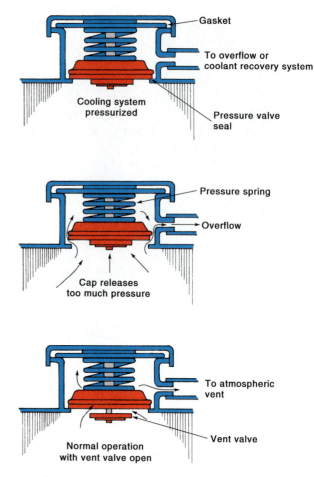

Figure 7–13 The operation of a typical pressure cap.

DIAGNOSTIC STORY

The Case of the Rusting Radiator Cap

During a routine service on a General Motors pickup truck, a service technician discovered that the entire cooling system was full of rust. See Figure 7–14. A search of technical service bulletins (TSBs) indicated that the rust is often caused by a lower level of coolant caused by a leak. When cast-iron parts of the engine are exposed to the oxygen in the air, they rust. This rust will then travel through the cooling system causing clogs or preventing the proper operation of the thermostat and radiator cap. The repair, according to the TSB, was to flush the system and refill with coolant. A careful analysis of this particular case indicated that the radiator cap seal had failed, allowing a loss of coolant, which then led to the rust problem.

Figure 7–14 A radiator cap from a truck that operated with a low coolant level.

Figure 7–15 A typical coolant recovery container.

cess coolant while the system is hot. See Figure 7–15. When the system cools, the pressure in the cooling system is reduced and a partial vacuum forms. This pulls the coolant from the plastic container back into the cooling system, keeping the system full. Because of this action, this system is called a **coolant recovery system.**

> **NOTE:** If you notice a radiator hose has collapsed when the engine cools, do not assume it is a bad hose. This collapse of the hose is a result of a defective radiator cap. A properly operating cap should draw coolant from the radiator overflow container back into the radiator and not form a vacuum in the system.

Frequently Asked Question ???

How Does the Pressure Cap Make the Water Pump More Efficient?

A problem that sometimes occurs with a high-pressure cooling system involves the water pump. For the pump to function, the inlet side of the pump must have a lower pressure than its outlet side. If inlet pressure is lowered too much, the coolant at the pump inlet can boil, producing vapor. The pump will then spin the coolant vapors and not pump coolant. This condition is called **pump cavitation.** Therefore, a radiator cap could be the cause of an overheating problem. A pump will not pump enough coolant if not kept under the proper pressure for preventing vaporization of the coolant.

TECH TIP ✔

Check the Radiator, Not the Overflow Container

If an engine is overheating or if the heater produces heat only once in a while, the coolant level should be checked. Many people check the level of coolant in the overflow container and believe that if the radiator were low, the coolant would be drawn from the overflow container into the radiator. However, if there is a leak from a defective water pump, for example, the cooling system will not be air tight and a vacuum will not be formed to draw coolant from the overflow back into the radiator.

Therefore, if there is a cooling system problem, always check the level of the coolant at the radiator itself. See Figure 7–16. Always check the coolant when the engine is cold or before the engine is started to avoid getting burned by hot coolant, which will gush from the radiator if the pressure cap is removed when the coolant is hot.

■ TESTING THE COOLING SYSTEM

Pressure Testing

Pressure testing using a hand-operated pressure tester is a quick and easy cooling system test. The radiator cap is removed (engine cold!) and the tester attached in the place of the radiator cap. By operating the plunger on the pump, the entire cooling system is pressurized. See Figures 7–17 and 7–18.

Figure 7–16 When checking the cooling system, always inspect the coolant level in the radiator itself, but never when the engine is warm. Always allow the engine to cool to room temperature before removing the radiator pressure cap.

Use Distilled Water in the Cooling System

Two technicians are discussing refilling the radiator after changing antifreeze. One technician says that distilled water is best to use because it does not contain minerals that can coat the passages of the cooling system. The other technician says that any water suitable to drink can be used in a cooling system. Both technicians are correct. If water contains minerals, however, it can leave deposits in the cooling system that could prevent proper heat transfer. Because the mineral content of most water is unknown, using distilled water, which has no minerals, is better. Although the cost of distilled water must be considered, the amount of water required (usually about 2 gallons [8 liters] or less of water) makes the expense minor in comparison to the cost of radiator or cooling system failure.

Figure 7–17 A typical radiator pressure tester set showing the various adapters needed to test different sizes of radiator cap openings.

Figure 7–18 Pressure testing the cooling system. A typical hand-operated pressure tester applies pressure equal to the radiator cap pressure. The pressure should hold; if it drops, this indicates a leak somewhere in the cooling system. An adapter is used to attach the pump to the cap to determine if the radiator can hold pressure, and release it when pressure rises above its maximum rated pressure setting.

CAUTION: Do not pump up the pressure beyond that specified by the vehicle manufacturer. Most systems should not be pressurized beyond 14 psi (100 kPa). If a greater pressure is used, it may cause the water pump, radiator, heater core, or hoses to fail.

If the cooling system is free of leaks, the pressure should stay and not drop. If the pressure drops, look for evidence of leaks anywhere in the cooling system including:

- Heater hoses
- Radiator hoses
- Radiator
- Heat core
- Cylinder head
- Core plugs in the side of the block or cylinder head

Pressure testing should be performed whenever there is a leak or suspected leak. The pressure tester can also be used to test the radiator cap by using an adapter to connect the pressure tester to the radiator cap. Replace any cap that will not hold pressure.

Coolant Dye Leak Testing

A coolant leak is normally identified as a grayish-white stain as shown in Figure 7–19. One of the best methods for checking for a coolant leak is to use a fluorescent dye in the coolant. Use a dye designed for coolant. See Figure 7–20. Operate the vehicle with the dye in the coolant until the engine reaches normal operating temperature. Use a black light to inspect all areas of the cooling system. When there is a leak, it will be easy to spot because the dye in the coolant will be seen as a bright green.

GRAYISH-WHITE STAIN

Figure 7–19 A coolant leak usually leaves a grayish-white stain.

■ THE WATER PUMP

Operation

The water pump is driven by a belt from the crankshaft or driven by the camshaft.

> **NOTE:** A water pump is also called a coolant pump.

Coolant recirculates from the radiator to the engine and back to the radiator. Low-temperature coolant leaves the radiator by the bottom outlet. It is pumped into the warm engine block, where it picks up some heat. From the block, the warm coolant flows to the hot cylinder head, where it picks up more heat.

> **NOTE:** Some engines today use **reverse cooling.** This means that the coolant flows from the radiator to the cylinder head(s) before flowing to the engine block. This results in cooling of the cylinder heads and allows for a high compression ratio and more advanced ignition timing without engine-damaging detonation (spark knock).

Water pumps are not positive displacement pumps. The water pump is a **centrifugal pump** that can move a large volume of coolant without increasing the pressure of the coolant. The pump pulls coolant in at the center of the **impeller.** Centrifugal force then throws the coolant outward so that it is discharged at the impeller tips. This can be seen in Figure 7–21.

As engine speeds increase, more heat is produced by the engine and more cooling capacity is required. The pump impeller speed increases as the engine

Figure 7–20 Use dye specifically made for coolant when checking for leaks using a black light.

Figure 7–21 Coolant flow through the impeller and scroll of a coolant pump for a V-type engine.

Figure 7–22 This severely corroded water pump could not circulate enough coolant to keep the engine cool. As a result, the engine overheated and blew a head gasket.

speed increases to provide extra coolant flow at the very time it is needed.

Service

A worn impeller on a water pump can reduce the amount of coolant flow through the engine. See Figure 7–22. If the seal of the water pump fails, coolant will leak out of the hole, often called a *weep* hole. The hole allows coolant to escape without getting trapped and forced into the water pump bearing assembly. See Figure 7–23.

If the bearing is defective, the pump will usually be noisy and will have to be replaced. Before replacing a water pump that has failed because of a loose or noisy bearing, be sure to do all of the following:

- Check the belt tension.
- Check for a bent fan.
- Check the fan for balance.

If the water pump drive belt is too tight, excessive force may be exerted against the pump bearing. If the cooling fan is bent or out of balance, the resulting vibration can damage the water pump bearing.

Figure 7–23 Cutaway of a typical water pump showing the long bearing assembly and seal. The weep hole is located between the seal and the bearing. If the seal fails, then coolant flows out of the weep hole to prevent the coolant from damaging the bearing.

■ RADIATOR COOLING FANS

Air is forced across the radiator core by a cooling fan. On older engines used in rear-wheel-drive vehicles, the fan is attached to a fan hub that is pressed on the water pump shaft. See Figure 7–24. In most installations in rear-wheel-drive and transverse engines, the fan is driven by an electric motor. See Figure 7–25.

NOTE: Most electric cooling fans are computer controlled. To save energy, most cooling fans are turned off whenever the vehicle is traveling faster than 35 MPH (55 km/h). The ram air at that speed should be enough to keep the radiator cool. Of course, if the computer senses that the temperature is still too high, it will turn the cooling fan on, to "high," if possible, in an attempt to cool the engine to avoid severe engine damage.

Figure 7–24 A typical engine-driven cooling fan.

Figure 7–25 A typical electric cooling fan assembly.

The fan is designed to move enough air at the lowest fan speed to cool the engine when it is at its highest coolant temperature. The **fan shroud** is used to increase cooling system efficiency.

THERMOSTATIC FANS

Since the early 1980s, most cooling fans have been computer-controlled electric motor units. On some rear-wheel-drive vehicles, the thermostatic cooling fan is driven by a belt from the crankshaft, so it turns faster as the engine turns faster. Generally, since the engine is required to produce more power at higher speeds, the cooling system must also transfer more heat at those speeds, which aids in the required cooling. Reducing engine heat becomes critical at low engine speeds in traffic when the vehicle is moving slowly.

The thermal fan is designed to use little power at high engine speeds and to minimize noise. It has a **silicone coupling** fan drive mounted between the drive pulley and the fan.

> **HINT:** Whenever diagnosing an overheating problem, look carefully at the cooling fan. If silicone is leaking, then the fan may not be able to function correctly and should be replaced.

A second type of thermal fan has a **thermostatic spring** added to the silicone coupling fan drive. The thermostatic spring operates a valve that allows the fan to freewheel when the radiator is cold. As the radiator warms to about 150° F (65° C), the air hitting the thermostatic spring will cause the spring to change its shape. The new shape of the spring opens a valve that allows the drive to operate like the silicone coupling drive. When the engine is very cold, the fan may operate at high speeds for a short time until the drive fluid warms slightly. The silicone fluid will then flow into a reservoir to let the fan speed drop to idle. See Figure 7–26.

HEATER CORE

Most of the heat absorbed from the engine by the cooling system is wasted, but some is recovered by the vehicle heater. Heated coolant is passed through tubes in the small core of the heater. Air is passed across the heater fins and then is sent to the passenger compartment. In some vehicles, the heater and air conditioner work in series to maintain vehicle compartment temperature.

HEATER PROBLEM DIAGNOSIS

When the vehicle's heater does not produce the desired amount of heat, many owners and technicians replace the thermostat before doing any other troubleshooting. It is true that a defective thermostat is the reason for the *engine* not reaching normal operating temperature. But many other causes besides a defective thermostat can result in lack of heat from the heater. To determine the exact cause, follow the procedure described below.

Figure 7–26 Cutaway of a viscous fan clutch showing the many grooves that are filled with viscous silicone fluid during operation.

(a)

(b)

Figure 7–27 (a) Many vehicles today use quick connect-type fittings on the heater hose. (b) The outside of the heater core housing showing one hose removed. Carefully inspect and clean these connections to prevent a leak.

With the engine running, feel both heater hoses. (The heater should be set to the maximum heat position.) Both hoses should be too hot to hold. If both hoses are warm (not hot) or cool, check the heater control valve for proper operation. If one hose is hot and the other (return) is just warm or cool, remove both hoses from the heater core or engine and flush the heater core with water from a garden hose. See Figure 7–27.

HINT: Heat from the heater that "comes and goes" is most likely the result of low coolant level. Usually with the engine at idle, there is enough coolant flow through the heater, but at higher engine speeds the circulation of coolant through the heads and block prevents sufficient flow through the heater.

■ COOLANT TEMPERATURE WARNING LIGHT

Most vehicles are equipped with a heat sensor for the engine operating temperature. If the "hot" light comes on during driving (or the temperature gauge goes into the red danger zone), the coolant temperature is about 250° to 258° F (120° to 126° C), which is still *below* the boiling point of the coolant (assuming a properly operating pressure cap and system). If this happens, follow these steps:

Step 1. Shut off the air conditioning and turn on the heater. The heater will help get rid of extra heat from the engine. Set the blower speed to high.

Step 2. If possible, shut the engine off and let it cool. (This may take over an hour.)

Highway Overheating

A vehicle owner complained of an overheating vehicle, but the problem occurred only while driving at highway speeds. The vehicle, equipped with a General Motors Quad 4, would run in a perfectly normal manner in city-driving situations. See Figure 7–28.

The technician flushed the cooling system and replaced the radiator cap and the water pump, thinking that restricted coolant flow was the cause of the problem. Further testing revealed coolant spraying out of one cylinder when the engine was turned over by the starter with the spark plugs removed.

A new head gasket solved the problem. Obviously, the head gasket leak was not great enough to cause any problems until the engine speed and load created enough flow and heat to cause the coolant temperature to soar.

The technician also replaced the oxygen (O_2) sensor because coolant contains silicone and silicates that often contaminate the sensor. The deteriorated oxygen sensor could have contributed to the problem.

Figure 7–28 When an engine overheats, often the coolant in the overflow container boils.

Step 3. Never remove the radiator cap when the engine is hot.

Step 4. Do *not* continue to drive with the hot light on, or serious damage to your engine could result.

Step 5. If the engine does not feel or smell hot, it is possible that the problem is a faulty hot light sensor or gauge. Continue to drive, but to be safe, stop occasionally and check for any evidence of overheating or coolant loss.

Quick-and-Easy Cooling System Problem Diagnosis

If overheating occurs in slow, stop-and-go traffic, the usual cause is low airflow through the radiator. Check for airflow blockages or cooling fan malfunctioning. If overheating occurs at highway speeds, the cause is usually a radiator or coolant circulation problem. Check for a restricted or clogged radiator.

■ BURPING THE SYSTEM

In most systems, small air pockets can occur. The engine must be thoroughly warmed to open the thermostat. This allows full coolant flow to remove the air pockets. The heater must also be turned to full heat. Some engines are equipped with a bleeder valve to allow air to escape when filling the cooling system with coolant. See Figure 7–29.

HINT: The cooling system will not function correctly if air is not released (burped) from the system after a refill. An easy method of doing this involves replacing the radiator cap after the refill, but only to the first locked position, and driving the vehicle for several minutes. With the radiator cap loosely sealed, no pressure can build up in the cooling system, and driving the vehicle helps circulate the coolant enough to force all air pockets up and out of the radiator filler. Top off the radiator after burping and replace the radiator cap to the fully locked position. Failure to burp the cooling system to remove all the air will often result in lack of heat from the heater and may result in engine overheating.

■ THE LUBRICATION SYSTEM

Oil Pumps

All production automobile engines have a full-pressure oil system in which oil is forced into the lubrication system under pressure. The pressure is maintained by an oil pump. See Figures 7–30 and 7–31.

In many engines, the distributor drive gear meshes with a gear on the camshaft, as shown in Figures 7–32 and 7–33. The oil pump is driven from the end of the distributor shaft, often by a hexagon-shaped shaft. Some engines have a short shaft gear that meshes with the cam gear to drive both the distributor and oil pump. In other engines, the oil pump is driven by the front of the crankshaft, in a setup similar to that of an automatic transmission pump,

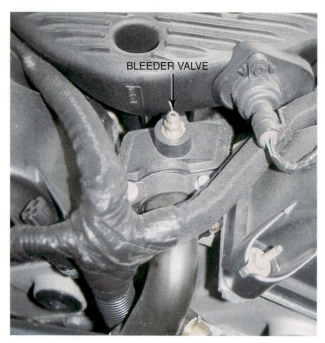

BLEEDER VALVE

(a)

(b)

Figure 7–29 (a) DaimlerChrysler recommends that the bleeder valve be opened whenever refilling the cooling system. (b) DaimlerChrysler also recommends that a clear plastic hose (1/4″ ID) be attached to the bleeder valve and directed into a suitable container to keep from spilling coolant onto the ground and on the engine and to allow the technician to observe the flow of coolant for any remaining air bubbles.

OIL PUMP

Figure 7–30 Cutaway of a Chevrolet V-8 engine showing the location of the oil pump.

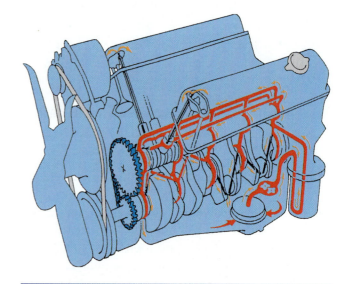

Figure 7–31 Typical V-8 engine lubrication system. Oil is stored in the oil pan (sump) and drawn into the oil pump and through the oil filter and on through the oil passages (oil galleries).